FORGOTTEN THINGS

TA▷ TEACHING ARCHAEOLOGY
Case Studies in Research and Fieldwork

Series Editor: Robert J. Muckle, Capilano University

Teaching Archaeology is an exciting new series of concise archaeological case studies that are engaging to read, manageable to teach, and flexible enough to be used in multiple courses. Books in the series provide students with real-world examples of the archaeological research process, as well as insights into the practical realities of doing fieldwork, including unexpected events, unplanned discoveries, logistical challenges, and reflections on ethics, collaboration, and the role of archaeology in the modern world. Each book includes photographs from the field and pedagogical features such as discussion questions, further readings, and a glossary of key terms.

FORGOTTEN THINGS

THE STORY OF THE SEYMOUR VALLEY ARCHAEOLOGY PROJECT

ROBERT J. MUCKLE

UNIVERSITY OF TORONTO PRESS
Toronto Buffalo London

© University of Toronto Press 2022
Toronto Buffalo London
utorontopress.com
Printed in the U.S.A.

ISBN 978-1-4875-8853-3 (cloth)   ISBN 978-1-4875-8854-0 (EPUB)
ISBN 978-1-4875-8852-6 (paper)   ISBN 978-1-4875-8855-7 (PDF)

Library and Archives Canada Cataloguing in Publication

Title: Forgotten things : the story of the Seymour Valley Archaeology Project / Robert J. Muckle.
Names: Muckle, Robert James, author.
Description: Series statement: Teaching archaeology | Includes bibliographical references and index.
Identifiers: Canadiana (print) 20220181845 | Canadiana (ebook) 20220181926 | ISBN 9781487588533 (cloth) | ISBN 9781487588526 (paper) | ISBN 9781487588540 (EPUB) | ISBN 9781487588557 (PDF)
Subjects: LCSH: Seymour Valley Archaeology Project. | LCSH: Archaeology – Research – British Columbia – Case studies. | LCSH: Archaeology – Fieldwork – British Columbia – Case studies. | LCSH: Lumber camps – British Columbia – History – 20th century – Case studies. | CSH: Japanese Canadians – British Columbia – History – 20th century – Case studies. | LCGFT: Case studies.
Classification: LCC CC165 .M79 2022 | DDC 930.1 – dc23

We welcome comments and suggestions regarding any aspect of our publications – please feel free to contact us at news@utorontopress.com or visit us at utorontopress.com.

Every effort has been made to contact copyright holders; in the event of an error or omission, please notify the publisher.

We wish to acknowledge the land on which the University of Toronto Press operates. This land is the traditional territory of the Wendat, the Anishnaabeg, the Haudenosaunee, the Métis, and the Mississaugas of the Credit First Nation.

University of Toronto Press acknowledges the financial support of the Government of Canada and the Ontario Arts Council, an agency of the Government of Ontario, for its publishing activities.

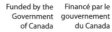

This book is dedicated to those largely forgotten people who lived in the forested and remote parts of the Seymour Valley during the early twentieth century, and to those 217 archaeology field school students who have worked to reveal the lives and cultures of those early residents.

Contents

Figures

Boxes

About This Book

ABOUT THE TITLE

"Forgotten Things" in the title of this book refers to abandoned places and things in that portion of the Seymour Valley in British Columbia where the Seymour Valley Archaeological Project has focused. While some of the remnants of historic places are known, the stories behind them have been forgotten. Conversing with people who lived in the area several decades ago, the project director triggered memories of forgotten things. All the archaeological sites mentioned in this book were deliberately abandoned: some by design and some forced. Some of the forgotten things were good (as when early residents of the valley were reminiscing about the good times of their youth in the valley, living in what are now the ruins of what the project has been documenting). Some of the forgotten things may have been deliberately repressed, such as the case of the Japanese Canadians who were likely living at one of the settlements until their forced removal to World War II internment camps. Because most of the sites were deliberately abandoned, most of the artifacts left behind were recognized as trash at the time. There is an exception though. One site, the focus of most of the fieldwork for the project, provides substantial evidence of people leaving many good and useable artifacts behind – dishes, clothing, and more. Some were hidden. We think the people intended to retrieve them but didn't. Eventually they were forgotten.

The title of this book is an homage to one of the classic books on historic archaeology in North America, by James Deetz. His book *In Small Things Forgotten: An Archaeology of Early American Life* (Deetz 1977) was short, engaging, highly readable, and informative to students, the public, and archaeologists – all things this book aspires to be.

ABOUT THE COVER IMAGE

The photo on the cover of this book shows artifacts on display at one of several archaeological sites studied during the Seymour Valley Archaeology Project. The site, known as the McKenzie Creek site, was established as a logging camp in the early 1900s but likely soon transitioned to a more permanent Nikkei (Japanese Canadian) settlement. The settlement was largely unknown, even to other residents living in the valley, and was likely abandoned during the forced evacuation of people of Japanese descent from the coastal areas of western North America during World War II. Following the site's abandonment, the forest soon hid evidence of the settlement, as natural processes covered artifacts and features. The kinds, quality, and condition of many artifacts suggest people intended to return to the site, but they never did. As with other sites investigated by the Seymour Valley Archaeology Project, the site and the artifacts were largely forgotten. The photo includes a sample of dishes and cosmetic jars as well as alcohol, ink, medicine, and milk bottles.

ABOUT THE AUTHOR

Robert Muckle has been practicing, teaching, and writing about archaeology for more than 30 years, with archaeology field experience in Canada, the United States, and Egypt. He once had his own commercial archaeology company working in advance of development projects and, for a few years, did archaeology exclusively in the service of First Nations. Capilano University in North Vancouver, Canada, is his work home. Although Robert is his official first name, he also answers to "Bob" and "Hey Muckle."

Most of his field research in the early decades of the twenty-first century has focused on the Seymour Valley Archaeology Project, described in this book. His archaeological interests remain wide, however, and include public archaeology, decolonizing archaeology, archaeology and popular culture, global prehistory, and the archaeology of the contemporary world.

Archaeology is full of bias, and it's important to recognize it. All of Muckle's archaeology professors were male; most were American, a few Canadian; and all were of European descent. Muckle too is of European descent. He consciously tries to counter the biases and privileges of his own that he is aware of and worries about those he is not; and in most cases, he respects the biases of others. He also likes to think he keeps current with recent developments in archaeology – methodological, theoretical, and ethical. He places strong value on public archaeology, on working in archaeology as a service to others, and on archaeology that furthers social justice.

When he started the project upon which this book is based, he was a mid-career archaeologist, still fairly new at the university teaching game; he had brown hair and was fit enough to hike, scramble up and down embankments, and leap over streams with his students, covering 20 km or more a day through the forest. Now, as this book goes to publication, he is a late-career archaeologist, the recipient of a long service award at Capilano University; he has white hair and struggles more with the hiking, scrambling, and leaping. He still loves fieldwork though, even in the rain.

He has won no awards for teaching, research, writing, or speaking; no national government has sought his advice (even though he has offered to give it); and if the Nobel Committee called, he must have missed it. He does take some pride, however, in having a judge of the Supreme Court of British Columbia recommend some of his work to lawyers, in having many former students go on to very successful and rewarding careers in archaeology and related fields, and in having received an award from the District of North Vancouver for his work on the Seymour Valley Archaeology Project.

Other books he has published with the University of Toronto Press include *Through the Lens of Anthropology: An Introduction to Human Evolution and Culture*, third edition (coauthored with Laura González and Stacey Camp, 2022); *Introducing Archaeology*, third edition (coauthored with Stacey Camp, 2021); and *The Indigenous Peoples of North America: A Concise Anthropological Overview* (2012). He also edited *Reading*

Archaeology (2008) for the University of Toronto Press. *The First Nations of British Columbia: An Anthropological Overview* was published by UBC Press (2014). He is also series editor of the University of Toronto Press's Teaching Archaeology series.

ABOUT THE SERIES

This book is part of the Teaching Archaeology series of case studies, published by the University of Toronto Press. Books in the series are designed to be concise and engaging to read, primarily for use in university courses but also of interest to others interested in archaeology. Besides focusing on the process of research, books also provide insight into the culture of archaeological fieldwork.

Preface

WHAT THIS BOOK IS ABOUT

This little book is about many things. At its core, it's about archaeology – how it is done, from the conceptualization of a project to its completion. But it's more than that. Much more.

The book is also about the culture of archaeology, especially fieldwork. It's about many things often discussed informally among archaeologists but rarely seen in print, such as anxieties, problems, logistics, failures, adaptability, ethics, working in inclement weather and in the company of bears. It's about how the discovery of an unexpected artifact or a comment from a visitor to a site can lead to a new trajectory of research. It's about the history of those of European ancestry and the history of those with Japanese ancestry in the early decades of the twentieth century in western Canada. It's about homesteading, logging, recreation, and a secret residential settlement on the margins of an urban area.

It's about collaboration and consultation – and the joys and tribulations of archaeology field schools. It's about the importance of archaeology and sharing. It's also about how to run archaeology projects with little or no budget.

This book is a case study. It is mostly about the process of archaeology and about the culture of fieldwork. The project upon which this book is based occurred in a forested valley in western Canada and was primarily focused on the early twentieth-century activities of both Euro-Canadians and Japanese Canadians in the valley. The location, time period, and research focus are not what drive the book, though. What drives the book is sharing the process of archaeological research and the culture of fieldwork.

The project upon which this book is based began with a phone call from an educational programmer wondering if the author of this book would be interested in supervising children at a summer camp; they would be looking for artifacts with metal detectors. The programmer and archaeologist decided to meet, and the Seymour Valley Archaeology Project was born. This book takes the reader from that initial call through 14 seasons of fieldwork between 2000 and 2019, and it documents making the artifacts and research meaningful and the eventual winding down of the project, including the disposition of collected artifacts and the archiving of project records.

WHO THIS BOOK IS FOR

The readership of this book is expected to be wide. The primary readers targeted are college and university students enrolled in introductory archaeology courses. For these students, the book provides an example of the process of archaeology and gives insight into the culture of fieldwork. It may also find a readership in other courses such as historic archaeology.

This book could easily be paired with most standard texts designed for introductory courses in archaeology that focus on archaeological methods. The most obvious and, in the view of the author, the best would be *Introducing Archaeology* (Muckle and Camp 2021) because it would be easy to link the two books (e.g., much of the material presented in this book could be used to exemplify or enhance the content of *Introducing Archaeology*). Of course, the author of this book is biased because he is a coauthor of the other.

The book is also expected to find a readership among the public. It is expected that many readers will be curious to see how archaeology is done, the process and adventure of archaeology. Many readers will presumably be interested in early twentieth-century history in British Columbia and the western United States, in general, as well as in the history of the Nikkei (Japanese Canadians and Japanese Americans).

The book will also likely be read by those practicing archaeology: some to see how other archaeologists work, some because they are interested in the region or in the other topics it covers, and some for fun – to read the stories and anecdotes.

A NOTE ABOUT TERMINOLOGY

Terms that readers may not be familiar with, or at least not familiar with in the way that archaeologists use them, are bolded the first time they appear in the book and included in the glossary.

Much of the research reported in the book describes sites and artifacts left by people with Japanese ancestry. These people are referred to as Nikkei (which generally refers to people of Japanese descent living outside of Japan) or Japanese Canadian. The terms may be considered interchangeable.

Significant portions of the book also describe sites and artifacts left by people with European ancestry. These people are primarily referred to as settlers or Euro-Canadians in this book. In other contexts, they may be referred to as "Whites."

There have been name changes over the course of this project. The study area is now within the boundaries of the Lower Seymour Conservation Reserve (LSCR), which in the early years of the project was known as the Seymour Demonstration Forest. The Lower Seymour Conservation Reserve is under the jurisdiction of the Metro Vancouver Regional District, which in the early years of the project was known as the Greater Vancouver Regional District. The project has been associated with Capilano University, which in the early years was Capilano College.

HOW THIS BOOK IS ORGANIZED

The book follows the basic plan of most archaeological research projects involving fieldwork. Chapter 1 describes the inception of the project and contextualizes it in archaeology, local history, and the creation of a collaborative model. Chapter 2 focuses on the creation of the research design and logistics. Chapters 3, 4, 5, and 6 describe fieldwork at specific sites; Chapter 7 focuses on how the fieldwork is made meaningful by lab work, interpretations, and sharing. Chapter 8 brings the work to a close, focusing on the winding down of the project. Each chapter has a box feature. Most of these discuss the culture of fieldwork.

Many other visitors have also made significant contributions. Local residents Kathy Stubbs and Irene Nemeth were among a group visiting one of the sites one day, and their questions led to perhaps the most significant discovery of the project – a Japanese bathhouse (see Chapter 5). Similarly, Sharon Villeneuve, who was visiting the McKenzie Creek site with her archaeologist daughter Suzanne Villeneuve, suggested that one area of the site, which I thought was likely the location of a cabin or small house, could have been a garden. She was right.

I am very grateful for the support of the Nikkei community, whose members have offered insight into the features and artifacts with a Nikkei presence. Paramount in this regard are Sherri Kajiwara (director and curator) and Lisa Uyeda (collections manager) at the Nikkei National Museum and Cultural Centre. Daien Ide (reference historian) at MONOVA, the Museum and Archives of North Vancouver, has also been very helpful.

I further acknowledge the Tsleil Waututh and the Squamish Nations. The archaeological project has taken place in their unceded territories. They offered their consent for fieldwork to occur in their territories, and for that, I am grateful.

Of course, I am also grateful to the good folks at the University of Toronto Press. This book was developed under the initial guidance of executive editor Anne Brackenbury. When Anne left the press, Carli Hansen took over guidance, providing suggestions, reminders, cajoling – all in a friendly and understanding manner – to bring this book to fruition. All my experiences with UTP, including those in editorial, production, and marketing, have always been excellent.

I am very grateful to the anonymous archaeologist reviewers of the initial proposal for this book and for their reviews of the completed manuscript. They made many useful suggestions. I am also grateful to Karen Taylor who copyedited the final manuscript, making me appear to be a better writer than I really am.

Dr. Katherine Cook, an archaeologist at the University of Montreal, created the original art for this book. I am in awe of Katherine's ability to take my ideas and words and transform them into drawings. I also appreciate the work of cartographer Eric Leinberger in creating the maps from my own sloppy sketches and notes. Several of the photos in this book were taken by students – Nikki Simon, Nadine Ryan, and Mark Galvani – and I am grateful for permission to use them. I am further grateful to those students who are in the images, although for privacy reasons they are not named.

The support of my family, including my wife Victoria and children Miriam, Esther, Cody, Jonathan, Tomas, and Anna, is also greatly appreciated. The entire Seymour Valley Archaeology Project, spanning more than 20 years and involving everything from creating the research design to writing this book, has been very much a passion project, and my wife and children have always been supportive, even when it took me away from home both physically and mentally. Special appreciation goes to Victoria who helped with the public programming, Tomas who helped with the fieldwork, and Anna who spent days during multiple field seasons helping with excavations and was a leader on many occasions with public programming.

prior to this project. Those that do exist were done by commercial archaeology companies, mostly in the 1990s and early 2000s, working in advance of development projects within the study area, such as for new filtration plants and recreational pathways. They have recorded no **archaeological sites**.

1

Beginnings

Caller: Hi, I'm an educational programmer planning a summer camp for kids and am wondering if you or any of your students would be interested in supervising kids using metal detectors to find and then dig things up.

Archaeologist: Umm. What you are proposing may be illegal and is certainly unethical. But tell me more.

INTRODUCTION

There are many ways an archaeological project can start. Some are driven purely by academic interests – a quest to find something out for pure research reasons, to describe or explain some part, large or small, of the human past. Other times, probably most, a project starts because of a potential threat to known and unknown archaeological sites from a development project; the developer is compelled by government to contract archaeologists.

Other times, such as with the Seymour Valley Archaeological Project, the start of a project is fortuitous. An opportunity presents itself, and the timing is right.

This project started with a phone call, part of which is quoted above. An educational programmer working in association with the Lower Seymour Conservation Reserve called Capilano University, the closest institution to the reserve, asking if any archaeologist or archaeology students would be interested in supervising children searching for and then excavating historic **artifacts**. The call was forwarded to the author of this book, who would go on to develop and direct the project.

The educational programmer was enthusiastic; the archaeologist who picked up the phone (me) less so, at least initially. The archaeologist offered to meet with the educational programmer in the LSCR that same day, and within a couple of hours, the Seymour Valley Archaeology Project was born.

Although enthusiastic, the educational programmer did not want to do anything unethical or illegal. I had some time that day, so we met in the reserve, which was only a few kilometers via dirt road from my office at Capilano University in North Vancouver. We toured areas of potential interest in the now heavily forested region, where it was likely some buried historic remains existed. Instead of a children's activity, we agreed that, under my direction, Capilano University would run an archaeology field school in the LSCR, and we would have a public education component to the project. The **Metro Vancouver Regional District**, which operated the reserve, would provide logistical support for public programming and fieldwork; Capilano University would provide the rest – including research design, crews for fieldwork, analysis, and reporting.

We collaborated on a proposal. The educational programmer took it to his people (higher-ups at the Metro Vancouver Regional District). After consulting with and receiving approval from my colleagues in the Anthropology Department at Capilano University, I took it to my higher-up (the dean), and within a few days of that initial phone call, the agreement was in place.

This book is mostly a narrative of the project. It's a case study in the process of archaeology, from the original idea for the project to the winding down. The start of the project is easy to trace to the initial phone call back in 1999. The first field season occurred in 2000, the most recent in 2019. These first few chapters provide the background, situating the project in place and time and contextualizing it within archaeology. This is followed by a focus on the fieldwork associated with locating and documenting the residential structures (e.g., houses, cabins, trails, and fences) created by communities (i.e., mostly **Euro-Canadian** communities) in the early decades of the twentieth century. This, in turn, is followed by three chapters focusing on the fieldwork at some **Nikkei** (i.e., **Japanese Canadian**) sites, which were totally un-expected discoveries. The final chapters concentrate on how the field-work is made meaningful and how the project came to an end.

Along the way, the book shows how archaeological research involv-ing fieldwork may be done – how to design research; consider and exe-cute logistics, such as obtaining permits; look for sites; and record and excavate them once they are discovered. Also discussed is how we in-terpret the things we find, and why. The book further provides insight into the culture of field archaeology; how archaeologists work, think, and behave.

SITUATING THE PROJECT

This section situates the project, describing the study area, outlining the time period of interest, and describing how it fits within the context of **archaeology**.

The Study Area

The study area is the Lower Seymour Conservation Reserve (LSCR), a forested area nestled in the Coastal Mountains, a range in the Pacific Northwest region of North America. It is on the margins of **Metro Van-couver**, which has a population of about 2.5 million people (Figure 1.1).

The LSCR is managed by the Metro Vancouver Regional District and is comprised of 5,668 hectares (about 57 square kilometers, 22 square miles, or roughly the size of about 14,000 football fields). The Seymour River runs southward through the center, fed by many creeks originat-ing on the forested slopes. The environment can be characterized as a **temperate rain forest**, dominated by second growth fir, cedar, and hemlock trees. Salmon spawn in the Seymour River, and wildlife such as deer and bears are plentiful. Cougars are occasionally sighted. There is also a wide variety of birds, including ravens, which is important to know when doing archaeology since they will often steal small shiny objects, such as keys to storage boxes, watches, and jewelry.

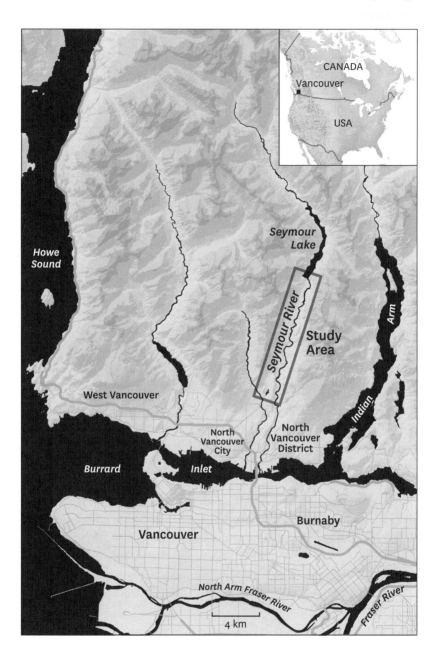

Figure 1.1. Map of the Study Area.

Vehicle traffic is restricted primarily to Metro Vancouver staff and to those associated with a fish hatchery or, fortunately, with archaeology. Despite restricted vehicle traffic, there are hundreds of thousands of visits to the LSCR each year for recreational activities, accommodated by about 120 km (75 miles) of trails for walking, hiking, and cycling.

The LSCR is immediately downstream of the Seymour Dam, which has created Seymour Lake. The lake provides water for about 40 per cent of the population of Metro Vancouver. Its capacity as a water reserve is what primarily defines the LSCR. Although not currently being used to store water, the LSCR does include infrastructure related to the water supply, water pipes, access roads, and a water filtration plant.

Although the LSCR is situated only about 10 km (6 miles) from Vancouver, one can easily get the feeling that it is a million miles away, such is the density of the forest, the sound of the river, and the lack of cell reception.

The main entrance and parking lot to the LSCR is about 5 km (3 miles) from Capilano University, the home base of the Seymour Valley Archaeology Project.

The LSCR has been featured in dozens of films and television series. Metro Vancouver has a well-established film and television industry, and many forest scenes are shot here. It was common during the field seasons to go through film sets. On one memorable day, field school students and I had to go through three different film sets to get to the site we were excavating. Students were particularly impressed one time when, traveling by vehicles along a dirt road to one of the remote sites in the forest, we came across filming on a bridge we had to cross. When we explained to the flag person who we were and where we needed to go, he immediately turned toward the crew on the bridge, repeatedly yelling, "Make way for the scientists! Make way for the scientists!" Apparently, the film crews were told that archaeology trumps filming. The smiles on the field school students' faces – because they had been called "scientists" and had made the film crews move – lasted hours. Sometimes film crews filmed very close to the archaeological sites we were excavating. At two different sites, we found evidence of small plastic leaves that blended into the vegetation. A bit of investigation revealed that they were part of camouflage for the equipment while filming.

Figure 1.2 is a map of the Lower Seymour Conservation Reserve (the study area) showing the location of the sites focused upon during the

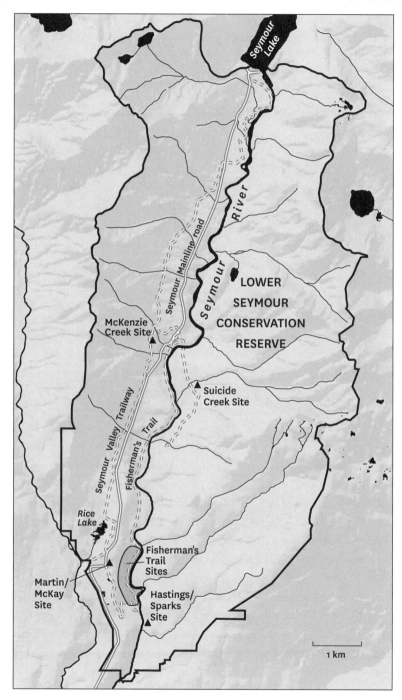

Figure 1.2. Map of Site Locations within the Study Area.

project. The Fisherman's Trail sites, the Hastings/Sparks site, and the Martin/McKay site are the focus of Chapter 3. The Suicide Creek site is the focus of Chapter 4, and the McKenzie Creek site is the focus of Chapters 5 and 6.

The Time Period of Interest

The period of interest for this project is from 1900 to 1950. Land use in the LSCR during this period was varied and included residential and recreational uses, logging, and, to a lesser degree, ranching and mining. There were also a few attempts at establishing commercial enterprises such as stores and places to have a cup of tea. A more complete history of the LSCR is provided later in this chapter.

Situating the Project within Archaeology

Most of the archaeology done in the Metro Vancouver area and the rest of British Columbia has focused on **prehistoric** sites, sometimes referred to as "precontact" or "precolonial" sites, which basically means that these sites involve settlements established before the arrival of Europeans in the area. Further, the **British Columbia Heritage Conservation Act** only offers automatic protection to sites older than 1846. Since most of the archaeology done in the province is **commercial archaeology**, for which there is little desire to document post-1846 sites, **historical archaeology**, or archaeology that focuses on cultural artifacts created when there were also written records, constitutes only a very small part of archaeology being done in the region. Historical archaeology *is* being undertaken though, increasingly every year, it seems.

Prior to the Seymour Valley Archaeology Project, there had been very little archaeological research undertaken in the study area. No academic archaeological research projects involving fieldwork had been undertaken. Some small-scale commercial archaeology projects (e.g., a few days of fieldwork) were done to assess the potential impact of construction within the LSCR. These projects were looking for pre-1846 sites. None were recorded. One of the reports did make a vague reference to a historic camp, which turned out to be a highly significant historic archaeological site. This is the McKenzie Creek site, the focus of Chapters 5 and 6 – and of much media attention (described in Chapter 7).

Besides historical archaeology, there are several other ways of contextualizing this project. It is an example of **academic archaeology** insofar as it has been driven by research questions and based out of a university. The project is also easy to see as an example of **community archaeology**. The project started with the explicit recognition that it *was* a community archaeology project, one serving primarily the needs of the local community of North Vancouver and secondarily those of the larger community of all of Metro Vancouver. While this kind of community archaeology remained a primary focus throughout, after the discovery of Nikkei sites, the notion of community archaeology was expanded to include the **descendant community** of Nikkei. This project is also an example of **public archaeology**, a type of archaeology often entangled conceptually with community archaeology. Public archaeology, which actively engages the public, has always been an important part of the project, often at the forefront.

Because the project focuses on the activities of non-Indigenous communities, it can also be considered a kind of **settler archaeology**. In this case, the settlers specifically referred to are the Euro-Canadians who made the Seymour Valley their home in the early twentieth century. Much of the focus of this project has been on the activities and sites of Nikkei, and, in this sense, the project fits within the area of **Asian American archaeology**.

The project may also be considered in the context of **collaborative archaeology**. The project has always been a collaborative effort between Capilano University and Metro Vancouver, but it is also collaborative in that it involved working with many diverse individuals, groups, and organizations, ranging from people who lived in the study area to foresters, geographers, descendant communities, museums, and other archaeologists.

While not as explicit and not as prominent, other kinds of archaeology are associated with the project. Because the project included excavations at three different sites where logging took place, it may be considered an example of **industrial archaeology**. The project has also included studies of activities and sites often associated with leisure and recreation: we found, for example, rental cabins for weekend and summer use, a bathhouse, gaming pieces, and part of a vinyl record, and we determined that a site had recently been used as an outdoor **marijuana growing operation (grow op)**. So the project may be considered as providing examples of the archaeology of leisure and recreation.

The project may also be considered within the realm of "field school archaeology." Field schools, which tend to be dominated by young adults in undergraduate programs, frequently bring sometimes-challenging sets of circumstances. For example, in addition to trying to teach and learn the methods of archaeology, participants are often navigating personal issues, conflicts, culture shock, immaturity, recklessness, and sometimes harassment and abuse. Within the realm of field school archaeology, this project is part of a subset known as "commuter field school archaeology," which means the project is local to the students; they live at home during the project and commute to the project study area daily.

This project is also an example of "low budget archaeology." Contrary to popular perceptions of archaeology and reports of archaeological research in mainstream media – which often depicts archaeologists using high-tech equipment, traveling to remote and exotic areas, driving flashy trucks, and having large crews – much archaeology is best described as "no budget" or "low budget" archaeology. This project clearly falls in this last category. The deal struck with the university at the inception of the project was that there would be no funding. We eventually did obtain bits, but it has always been a struggle. Over the years, we've had to borrow equipment, bend the rules, rummage through scraps, and be innovative – such as the time a student traded a case of beer for enough wood to build shoring for a wide and deep excavation unit.

THE PROJECT MODEL

The model, as initially conceived at its inception and maintained throughout the entire 20+ years of the project, is that the project would be collaborative. Capilano University would provide the project director (me) and fieldworkers (archaeology field school students), and it would have primary responsibility for archaeology field equipment and supplies, creating a research design, laboratory work, analysis, interpretation, and report writing. The project would have a substantial public education component, part of which involved plugging into the existing public education programs offered by Metro Vancouver, for which we developed K–12 activities, resources for summer children's camps, and public presentations.

The contributions of Metro Vancouver mostly involved providing logistical support. Besides the support offered in public programs, such as advertising, registration, and providing venues, logistical support included providing vehicle access (for only the project director to transport equipment, supplies, and more into and out of the sites where we were working each day). Metro Vancouver also liked the project director to have a vehicle on site in case of an emergency, such as a wildlife encounter gone bad. Additionally, Metro Vancouver provided keys to get through locked gates, vehicle transport for students via a small bus to a remote part of the LSCR (over multiple seasons), and portable toilets close to fieldwork locations. It also waived the permit fees for use of the LSCR.

Fieldwork was to be done primarily by students enrolled in Capilano University's Archaeology Field School, for which the project director (me) was the instructor. The details were negotiated with the dean at the inception of the project. The normal class size for an archaeology course was 35, and we agreed the field school would have only 15.

It was suggested that, as is very common elsewhere, there be a surcharge to students for the extra costs associated with the archaeology field school. I was steadfast in my refusal to allow a surcharge. I wanted the field school to be an opportunity for any student and not limit participation to students able and willing to pay more.

It was decided that rather than being worth the normal three credits for a course, the field school would be worth six credits. Because it was local, we decided to make the field school a commuter field school, which meant that the students would be responsible for getting themselves to and from the study area each day.

Finally, we decided that the anthropology department would choose the students. And we chose wisely. The field school was to run Monday to Friday for the seven-week condensed term in May and June.

The dean viewed the project as a pilot project the initial year, and hesitated to commit to more than one field season. Subsequent planning was always on a year-to-year basis. Overall, through the entire project, the administration was highly supportive of the project, recognizing its value to students and the university.

PROJECT OBJECTIVES

As the project continued long past the one season initially agreed upon, new discoveries led to new interests and shifting directions. The core objectives never changed though. Those core objectives center on the principal project components of education, research, and cultural

Figure 1.3. Principal Project Components. Credit: K. Cook.

resource management. Figure 1.3 is a sketch of the project director (on the right) with a student as both sift through excavated remains. The dishes depicted in the drawing are Japanese ceramics from one of the sites, and the map shows one of the sites investigated.

Education has two components. One is university training in the methods and culture of field archaeology. Almost all professional archaeologists obtain their first archaeological fieldwork experience as part of a field school. It is very much a rite of passage in archaeology. The second component is public education, which has guided much of the work of the project and facilitated the introduction of the process and results of archaeological research to many thousands of people. One of the educational objectives, categorized under this educational component, was to amplify the value of archaeology to the public. Box 1.1 describes that value, both in general and in terms of this particular project.

Initially, the research component simply focused on documenting some locally known but undocumented historic ruins in the LSCR, for example, by following up on evidence of old cabins. Simple documentation remained an important objective of the research throughout the project, with a goal to document sites to the standards set by

BOX 1.1 WHY ARCHAEOLOGY?

Early in the Seymour Valley Archaeology Project, the project director (me) participated in a meeting about the heritage of the Lower Seymour Conservation Reserve. At the meeting, besides myself, were Metro Vancouver staff, members of local heritage societies, professionals in the heritage industry, and members of the public – about two dozen people in total.

At one point, the discussion turned to the Seymour Valley Archaeology Project, and I gave a brief overview of what we were doing, why we were doing it, what our results so far were, and what our plans were. It hit a nerve. One person was incensed, saying, "I see no reason in having an archaeologist involved. There is no value they could bring. At most, if archaeologists are involved, they should only be allowed to dig where historians tell them to dig to confirm what the historians already know." I was surprised, but perhaps shouldn't have been, that this person saw such little value in archaeology.

Historical research, relying mostly on written documents, is one way of studying the past, but it is certainly not the only way. Archaeological research may be viewed as a complementary way of investigating the recent human past, whether in the Seymour Valley or anywhere else in the world. They are different, but one is not necessarily better than another.

Archaeology relies on the physical remains of human activities as the primary data source. In practical terms, this mostly means archaeologists look for and study physical evidence of places where people were, including evidence of structures (often referred to as **features**) and the smaller items they left behind (often called artifacts). It's a different way to look at the past, and it produces a different perspective from that achieved through historical research, which relies on written documents.

When doing historical archaeology, archaeologists can, and often do, familiarize themselves with historical documents. In the Seymour Valley Archaeology Project, for example, much historical research was done, both prior to the first excavations and continuing throughout. The historical research was important, but it was supplemental to searching for and studying the physical remains of human activities.

Archaeology provides a different perspective. It provides a more complete picture of the historical period than can be offered by looking at documents alone. Archaeologists know, for example, that not everything is documented. Many of the sites discovered and examined during the Seymour Valley Archaeology Project were never documented. There are no written accounts. It is impossible to even attempt to write a complete and unbiased history without archaeology in this circumstance. For example, the standard histories of the Seymour Valley, as for many areas, are focused on resource exploitation. There is little or no reference to the social and political contexts of people: how they lived, what their homes or their social lives were like, what gender or identity structures they had, and more. Especially, the Nikkei communities were almost totally neglected by the standard histories.

Archaeology is supported by governments throughout the world. Every country in the world has laws protecting archaeological sites and permit systems to ensure archaeological work is done properly. This is because it is valued.

Archaeology can **ground-truth** written histories – providing physical evidence of what documents suggest. Presumably, the person speaking at that meeting valued archaeology at least for its ability to check the "facts" of history. Historical archaeology can do that and does do that. Part of the Seymour Valley Archaeology Project has done that. But archaeology can do more, much more.

Archaeology is particularly good at bringing the activities of marginalized people to light. In the Seymour Valley Archaeology Project, this is mostly to do with Nikkei. In the early twentieth century, they were very much marginalized in the region. There was considerable racism. They were forcibly evacuated from the area. Much Nikkei history has been lost and forgotten, consequently.

The Seymour Valley Archaeology Project demonstrates the value of archaeology. It has provided a more complete picture of early twentieth century life in the valley – of who its residents and workers were and where and how they lived; it has confirmed some of the written and oral histories; and it has expanded on them. It has documented some known but undocumented places where people were living, working, and playing. It has discovered and documented multiple previously undocumented camps, and it has brought to light details of the experience of Nikkei in the valley, which has largely gone unrecorded in written histories.

the provincial government for recording archaeological sites. As the project continued, new discoveries led to new research objectives, and we started asking other research questions: How old are these sites? What were people doing here? When did they leave? Why did they leave? What was the ratio of males to females? Were children at the site? And many more questions besides. Research objectives further included creating a more complete record of local history and making scholarly contributions to archaeology.

Education and research have been the components that have driven much of the project, but there are also elements of **cultural resource management (CRM)**. Although restricted primarily to the public for recreational use only, the LSCR has seen a significant amount of development. It has been developed for infrastructure related to the water supply (e.g., through the construction of filtration plants, water pipe systems, and access roads) and for recreation (e.g., through the building and maintaining of trails for walking, hiking, and biking). So Metro Vancouver could make informed decisions about future development in the area, decisions that may impact historic archaeological sites, project objectives included not only documenting but also assessing the significance of some of the sites the project investigated.

A BRIEF HISTORY OF ACTIVITIES IN THE LSCR, 1900–1950

This section provides a brief overview of the history of the Lower Seymour Conservation Reserve, focusing on the time period of primary interest for this project: 1900 to 1950.

The start and end dates were chosen arbitrarily. As mentioned in the Introduction, it is close to certain that Indigenous peoples have been active in the valley for a very long time, beginning several thousand or more years ago and continuing to the present. Such is the nature of much of the writing of histories, particularly local histories, however, that the contributions of Indigenous peoples are left out. These histories instead focus on people of European descent, especially men. Such are the foci of most of the written histories of the Seymour Valley and surrounding areas.

What we do know is that the valley began to be exploited for resources by non-Indigenous people in the 1870s. Principally, this was for logging, and logging continued to be a primary activity in the valley until the 1920s. The late 1880s also saw the construction of the **Lillooet Trail** through a portion of the area, and some attempts at gold mining occurred in the late 1800s. Settlement that involved the construction of houses began in the late 1800s, but was likely limited to a dozen or fewer houses.

The early decades of the twentieth century saw the building of the Seymour Dam, continued logging, an increase in settlement, and the beginning of the use of the area for recreation. Rental cabins, stores, and snack shops were constructed, for example. The area was never densely populated. There was a small community along the western banks of the Seymour River comprising several houses and cabins. Scatterings of houses were also built elsewhere, near Rice Lake in the southern portion of the reserve and, in the northern part, near the dam. Cabins, mostly undocumented and for recreational use, began appearing elsewhere, especially on the eastern side of the river. Several local histories mention logging camps in the valley, but none offers precise locations.

As for the settlers, they were without electricity and running water for the most part. They were about an hour's walk through the forest to the closest transit stop. The kids walked to school in the neighboring valley, about an hour's walk each way.

Ostensibly to protect the water supply, commercial activity and settlement in the area started being curtailed in the 1940s. The Greater Vancouver Water District began buying the houses of residents. Those who wouldn't sell had their properties expropriated. All structures that could potentially offer shelter were burned, destroyed by other means, or dismantled and moved. By 1950 (or 1951, according to some), all the purchases and expropriations were complete, and the area now known as the Lower Seymour Conservation Reserve was closed to the public.

During the closure from 1950 to 1987, the forest took over, burying most of what little evidence of the historic period activities was left behind. The burning and demolition of structures had removed 95 per cent or more of the surface evidence of historic activities. Falling leaves and branches, eventually turning to litter mat and then soil, combined with the growth of vegetation on the forest floor made the historic activities nearly invisible, so much so that many people are still surprised when they learn that there were any camps or settlements in the area. Since the reopening of the area to public in 1987, for recreation use only, what little evidence remained on the surface has continued to disappear. Some of it has decomposed and some gets covered a bit more each year with falling leaves and the development of new soils.

As the years go by and the physical evidence of the historic period activities becomes less and less visible, the things that people had and left in the area are forgotten, as are the stories these things can tell. This is where the Seymour Valley Archaeology Project comes in – with its aim to find those things buried and forgotten, and to tell the stories.

2

Finding Our Way

Archaeological research projects are always guided by research design, unless amateurs are undertaking them.

– *Muckle and Camp (2021, 99)*

INTRODUCTION

This chapter is about finding our way, both metaphorically and literally. It's metaphorical in the sense of figuring out how to even start. How does one get approval from the university to undertake such a venture? How can the project director make the transition from doing prehistoric archaeology to doing historical archaeology? Develop and run a field school? Choose students? How does one run the project with no equipment and no budget? And there are many more questions. It's also literal in the sense of addressing specific, practical needs. How do we get to the study area each day? How do we navigate without maps and compasses, and in areas where there is no cell phone reception?

The opening epigraph makes the distinction between professional and most amateur archaeology. Professional archaeologists always have a plan before they start fieldwork. It is understood that plans can be tweaked or shift depending on what is found or what hurdles come up, but creating a **research design** is fundamentally important. This is quite unlike what many amateur archaeologists, often referred to as **pothunters**, do in which the endgame is usually the discovery of artifacts.

THE PROJECT SPIRAL

One of the things about archaeology is that you rarely know for sure what you will discover once you start digging. Figure 2.1 illustrates the spiral the Seymour Valley Archaeology Project took, one that widened from a narrowly defined center. It started as a one-field-season-only project focusing on known historic period residences. From there it spiraled out, generating interest and further field seasons. These further field seasons generated new interests and new research questions, and so on. The new interests and research questions led to new kinds of work being done in both the field and the lab. It was difficult to keep the project focused. Many people wanted to influence the project's direction – some wanted the project to expand the fieldwork into other valleys and communities; others wanted to focus on only Euro-Canadian or only Nikkei settlements.

CREATING A RESEARCH DESIGN: FINDING OUR METHODOLOGICAL COMPASS

As described by Muckle and Camp (2021, 99), "Research designs are critical for a variety of reasons. Most importantly, they establish (i) the significance of the project, (ii) the kinds of information being sought, (iii) the preferred methods for obtaining that information, and (iv) the plan for making the research meaningful."

There are nine basic stages of projects that involve the discovery and excavation of archaeological sites. These include, as described by Muckle and Camp (2021, 100),

- Identifying the objectives for research
- Background research
- Formulating hypotheses or research questions
- Determining the kinds of data to collect

Figure 2.1. The Project Spiral. Credit: K. Cook.

- Determining the field and laboratory methods to use
- Detailing the logistics to make the project work
- Collecting data
- Making the data meaningful
- Making the research meaningful

The following sections outline each stage. The research design has been very much a kind of living document. Initially, the project was approved for only a single year, and the original research design reflected that. As the project continued, alterations were made. New discoveries led to new questions, new objectives, new methods, and more. Each of the following sections presents a summary – sometimes organized into overall project components (education, research, and cultural resource management) – of how the initial research design planned to handle each step. Some of the subsequent changes to the research design are also summarized.

Identifying the Objectives for Research

As described in Chapter 1, the objectives for the Seymour Valley Archaeology Project center on education, research, and cultural resource management. Following approval of the project on that basis, the next stage in the development of the project was to flesh out these objectives. With the initial requirement that the project was to be for only one year, and with virtually no equipment or supplies, it was decided that there would be a surface survey only, no excavation. It was decided to focus on areas that were known, but not properly documented, and to survey areas suitable for public education with K–12 groups. In practical terms, this meant that the project would focus on areas with high **archaeological visibility** and easy access.

Objectives related to education included field school students being trained to a level that would meet or exceed the academic standards of undergraduate field schools elsewhere and also meet the needs of commercial archaeology companies looking for students to hire with fieldwork experience. There would be no excavation experience, but students would learn how to do archaeological survey work, as well as how to identify, record, and map archaeological sites. They would also become familiar with the culture of fieldwork. In subsequent years, teaching and learning excavation techniques were added to the objectives for training university students.

Regarding the public education component, it was decided that the project would plug into the existing programs being offered in the LSCR. This meant that we would offer archaeological programming to visiting K–12 school groups. In subsequent years, the public education component was expanded, with the objectives of increasing both the diversity and numbers of people reached. Programs expanded to include adults and a wide variety of community groups. We made presentations at community events, gave public lectures, held public excavation days, and blogged.

The initial objectives related to research were quite simple. Initially, the primary objective was to record known historic period sites in an area along the Seymour River known as the "homestead area." A secondary objective was to search for and document other historic sites in that area.

As the project continued, the number of research objectives increased. The discovery of new sites led to new questions. In subsequent years, objectives included determining answers to many new questions. How old is this site? When did it originate and for what purpose? Why was it abandoned? How many people lived there? What was their ethnic identity? What was the ratio of males and females at the site? Were children present? What were they eating? What was the relationship between sites?

Regarding cultural resource management, the initial objective was simply to make the results of our documentation available to Metro Vancouver so that staff could make informed decisions. In subsequent years, a significant addition to the cultural management component included assessments of the significance of the sites. Criteria for assessing **site significance** are included in Appendix 2. Subsequent years also saw the inclusion of a new objective: adding information on the sites to the heritage management plans for the LSCR.

Background Research

The initial background research on the project involved reviewing **archaeological impact assessment** reports done within the LSCR and archaeological reports about nearby areas, reading several regional and local histories of the area, reviewing ethnographic information on local First Nations, and becoming familiar with the landscapes of the LSCR.

In subsequent years, historical and archival research continued. When Nikkei camps were discovered, background research on Nikkei history and Japanese American archaeology became intense. We never expected to discover Nikkei sites, and we needed to become familiar with Nikkei local history in a hurry.

Formulating Hypotheses or Research Questions

Original research questions were simple. For example, how many known historic period sites will we be able to record properly? We hypothesized that we could record several in that first year. In subsequent years, as we began to discover new sites, mostly related to Nikkei, we had other research questions. "When was the Nikkei site occupied?" is a good example. As we continued, we started forming hypotheses: "This site was deliberately abandoned because logging was no longer sustainable" and "Once logging ceased in the area, the Nikkei transitioned this site from a logging camp to a secret residential camp, which they occupied until forced evacuation in 1942."

Determining the Kinds of Data to Collect

During the initial field season, the data we wanted to collect were simple. We wanted to record features and artifacts on the ground surface. We also wanted to collect stories and memories of people who lived in the study area during the time of interest (1900–50). In subsequent years, we added information on subsurface features and artifacts to the kind of data we wanted to collect. We also recorded the botanical and animal remains we discovered in cultural context and soil samples.

To test hypotheses, such as "This site was deliberately abandoned" or "This was a forced evacuation," we collected data on the kinds of artifacts left behind. Large numbers of dishes and other artifacts in good condition would support forced evacuation. This is discussed more fully in Chapter 7.

One of the issues facing many archaeologists is how to define "archaeological sites" and "artifacts." There are some fairly standard, comprehensive definitions of sites, such as there must be physical evidence of human activity to qualify as a site. And (at least in North America) an artifact must be portable and exhibit evidence of physical use. When beginning archaeology projects, however, archaeologists usually figure out how to operationalize these definitions. We asked, for example, under what circumstances would we describe an area as a site? What are the minimum requirements of being described as a site? For the Seymour Valley Archaeology Project, we established that we were going to use 1950 as the cut-off. We would not classify as a site any physical evidence of human activity that postdated 1950. Our classification was further judgmental in that we used judgmental site sampling; we knew, for example, that looking for sites in areas where there was a high probability of our finding them meant that it would not be valid to use the number of sites we found to estimate the total number of sites in the study area. Determining how to classify items as artifacts before we began fieldwork was also problematic. This was, at least in part, because we had little idea of what to expect.

The definition of artifact remained flexible in subsequent years. Near the beginning, for example, we defined every nail and piece of bottle glass or broken piece of a ceramic dish as an artifact. This definition became unwieldy, though, so we found ourselves occasionally redefining "artifact." For example, we decided eventually that to be considered an artifact a piece of bottle glass or a **potsherd** needed to have some diagnostic characteristic that could tell us something about age, location of origin, or function.

Determining the Field and Laboratory Methods to Use

Field methods have always been restricted by budget. This was of little consequence in the initial years when most of the work was limited to documenting known historic features and artifacts scattered on the ground surface. It was simple enough. We would go to the area and document, with pencils and paper, what we found. The techniques for **survey** never changed substantially during the project. We used Google Earth in subsequent years to look for potential areas to investigate, but use of this technology was limited since the project's objectives were never to undertake a comprehensive survey. Mostly, we used Google Earth to look for changes in vegetation around sites we had already discovered, changes that may have resulted from the creation and use of old logging roads or pathways. We also looked at archival maps of the LSCR to see where potential sites might be and relied heavily on consultation with former residents of the area and staff of the LSCR.

Students had to learn how to read topographic maps. In the early years of the project, before **GPS** technology became widely available and affordable, it was important that students be able to use maps to survey areas, locate themselves on a map, and identify the precise latitude and longitude coordinates on a map. As a standard, we used the 1:50,000 scale maps produced by Natural Resources Canada to conform to the National Topographic System (NTS). Of course, as GPS became ubiquitous, our reliance on maps diminished. Most students, though, were still required to learn how to read the maps.

Once the project added excavations, it was decided to keep the excavation methods simple, by design. We used test pits and excavated in 2-meter by 2-meter square units (1 meter equals 1.09 yards; excavation is almost always done using the metric system). And we established **arbitrary levels** (i.e., we kept track of things according to predetermined levels, such as at every 5 or 10 cm of depth; 5 cm is approximately 2 inches). Things were kept simple for two reasons: (i) none of the students had excavation experience, so it would have been too difficult and slow to excavate by **natural levels** (i.e., excavating and keeping track of things based on differences in the sediments, such as color and texture); and (ii) since we were focusing on early twentieth century deposits, we expected the cultural deposits to be shallow. Two-meter square excavation units were chosen to foster collaboration with students in the sense that there would be enough room for two people to work together in the same unit. Also, this is a standard size excavation unit for many archaeological projects in the region.

When excavating distinct features, rather than excavating in 2-meter by 2-meter units, we chose to excavate by the boundaries of the feature itself. This was mostly relevant to the excavations at the McKenzie Creek site (see Chapters 5 and 6).

Lack of budget precluded having a **total station**, so we used compasses, provided by the geography department. We used 30-meter tapes, and students learned the length of their pace (i.e., the length of their stride).

Going paperless during fieldwork, during both surveys and excavations, is a recent trend in archaeology. There simply was no budget for GPS equipment and total stations that record information, nor was there a budget for portable devices such as laptops.

Because project participants relied on paper field notes, using paper maps and handheld compasses, and measuring distances without a total station, they were often told, "Should you ever be on a future project when all the batteries die, you will be the go-to person on the project. Finding coordinates on a map, no problem. Finding horizontal and vertical distances, no problem. Setting up 2-meter by 2-meter excavation units, no problem."

Logistics

Logistics includes many things that may be considered administrative. For most projects, logistical work means obtaining funding, permits, and permissions; obtaining field equipment and supplies; and arranging travel, food, and accommodation for the crew. For the Seymour Valley Archaeology Project, because fieldwork was being done within a commuter field school, arranging travel, accommodation, and food required little logistical work. Obtaining equipment and supplies with no budget was the biggest concern.

As is the case with almost all archaeological field projects in North America, at the start of the project, logistical considerations included obtaining appropriate permits and permissions. With the approval of Metro Vancouver and Capilano University already in place, I turned my attention to obtaining a permit from the provincial government to undertake the project. Legislation in British Columbia requires permits for archaeological projects involving the excavation of pre-1846 sites to be in place (these are issued by the British Columbia Archaeology Branch). Since the project was focusing on the early twentieth century, there was no need for a permit from the government. The project director assumed the government would still like to know about the project, but he was wrong. The project director applied for a permit, but the response from government was "We can send the application back to you, or shred it." I chose shredding.

Although notifying potentially affected Indigenous peoples was not required or common practice, before starting the project, I wrote letters to the two local First Nations – the Tsleil Waututh and the Squamish Nations – informing them what we planned to do. I told them that the project was focusing on only early twentieth century sites associated with settler residences and that if we discovered any sites indicative of Indigenous use, I would stop immediately and consult with them. In the years since the start of the project, First Nations throughout the region initiated their own permit systems to do archaeological work in their territories. It is not required by provincial legislation that archaeologists obtain such permits, but obtaining them is common. In the latter stages of the project, after local First Nations established their own permitting systems, we obtained permits from those nations.

In the early years of the project, there was no need to obtain a permit from Metro Vancouver to work in the LSCR, but eventually there was. The fee was waived, but there was still a requirement to show proof of several million dollars of liability insurance. The university, through the provincial government, was able to provide evidence of this insurance for the project, at no cost.

Obtaining equipment and supplies without an official budget was a challenge. We were able to make some initial purchases by using part of the small departmental budget as well as parts of the unused budget for the School of Social Sciences, never identifying these purchases as being specifically for the field school. Fortunately, nobody ever asked why social scientists needed shovels, tarps, and flagging tape. We were also fortunate that other departments were willing to help. Geography gave us compasses as well as equipment and supplies for soil analysis. Horticulture let us use the departmental van to transport equipment and supplies to the sites daily. Facilities (the administrative department responsible for the operation and maintenance of the campus, including buildings, at Capilano) also let us use its trucks for transport.

One field season, an administrator visiting the excavations learned we were working in the company of bears. She asked how we dealt with that. I answered, "We just use common sense. I would like to have bear spray, but there is no budget." Without any further discussion, I received an email the next week indicating there was now a budget to purchase bear spray.

Almost every year, I put in a capital budget request to the university for an archaeology truck – nothing too fancy, preferably a four-wheel drive pickup to navigate old logging roads and trails, with a large enough box to transport equipment. It would have been fantastic to have the truck approved, but I really didn't think it would be. I was really hoping for approval of smaller-cost items, reasoning that the committees and administrators adjudicating the requests would have a good laugh at the request for a truck and then allow the smaller requests for shovels and such because they were in a good mood. I'm not sure how effective the strategy was, but we were able to get approval for relatively low-cost items.

Finding storage space was challenging. Capilano University is a teaching-focused university, not well suited to supporting research needing physical space. Storage space usually alternated between the small anthropology lab designed for storing teaching materials and abandoned rooms in other buildings. For some years, the storage space for equipment, supplies, and artifacts was in an abandoned and condemned building on campus. More specifically, storage was in a locked space that was once the shower area within – according to the sign on the door – the "Women's Change Room." It was a great place for storage, but unfortunately it was temporary. The building was demolished.

Collecting Data: The Field School Model

As mentioned in Chapter 1, enrollment for the field school was set at 15 students, and it would be a commuter field school running for seven weeks in May and June.

From the outset, the objective was to teach students and provide them with experience in both archaeological field methods and the culture of field archaeology. The project attempted to instill a strong archaeological work ethic in students. Because of our locale, field archaeology students would also become accustomed to working in the rain and in the company of bears, discussed in Box 2.1.

The field school ran for 14 field seasons from 2000 to 2019. Typically, we were in the field Mondays through Thursdays and on campus on Fridays. Students got themselves to and from the work areas on their own each day. They could take public transit or drive to the parking lot of the LSCR. The length of time it took to walk through the forest to and from the sites where we were working varied, ranging from 10 minutes to 60 minutes. Biking was an option for some. Because of the ever-present danger of bears and cougars, and to foster a collaborative model, students were always required to walk or bike to the sites with others.

Fridays were reserved for being on campus. We did some lab work on that day, but mostly Fridays were reserved for other things. Activities included some formal teaching about techniques, perhaps a technique that would be employed the following week or one that the director had noticed some students having difficulty with. The director would also provide a debriefing of the week that was, bringing students up to speed on the project's recent developments, giving them the big picture, and describing what the director was thinking. The director also provided a plan for the next week. There was always a weekly round table discussion focusing on student's individual contributions; at that table, we discussed what each student had been doing and thinking during the week. All of this was to foster a collaborative model.

Students were required to provide some of their own field equipment, including trowels and rain gear. They were strongly advised to

BOX 2.1 WORKING IN THE RAIN AND IN THE COMPANY OF BEARS

Every region has things that become part of the local culture of field archaeology. In the Pacific Northwest, particularly in coastal areas, those things include working in the rain and in the company of bears.

Working in the Rain

It rains a lot in the region. There is a saying in Metro Vancouver: "If you can see the mountains, it's going to rain. If you can't see the mountains, it's already raining." Rain is something that archaeologists just deal with in the area, usually without complaint. Students were told about working in the rain prior to submitting applications. Somehow, it wasn't real for some though. A few students had anticipated a career in archaeology until they experienced working in the rain. Anecdotally, the project director saw a correlation between rainy days and increased excavation productivity. It may be that, on those rainy days, students simply became more focused, leaning into their work. The rain also worked to expose some artifacts, especially bottles close to the surface. One day, when the rains were particularly heavy, the crew was surveying a historic homestead. While we were there, a raindrop exposed a 1923 dime. When we talked later with a man who had lived in the area in the 1930s, he claimed it was his, that he had lost it in his youth. At first, he asked for it back but then said it was okay to keep it in the collection. None of the 217 students ever vocally complained about working in the rain, at least not in a voice loud enough for the project director to hear. Some seemed to enjoy it. And it wasn't like it rained all the time. At one extreme, during one seven-week season there were only two days with traces of rain. At the other extreme, there was one season with only two days *without* traces of rain. On average, we experienced traces of rain on about 35 per cent of our days in the field. During one rainy field season, there was one student who always wore white sneakers, even in the rain. At the end of each rainy day, when everyone else was muddy and wet, we would all notice his unblemished white sneakers. Nobody could ever figure that out. One of the great mysteries of the Seymour Valley Archaeology Project!

Working in the Company of Bears
There are bears in the Seymour Valley. Lots of them. Like working in the rain, working in the company of bears is part of the local culture of field archaeology. Before submitting formal applications to the field school, students were told that it was reasonable to expect bears around – and that having bears nearby would not stop us from working. Bears were seen almost every field season, and sometimes they were very close to the sites. During one field season, one bear was a constant presence for a week, staying about 100 meters (110 yards) south of the site. During the same week, another bear was a constant presence about 150 meters (165 yards) north of the site. Students were all advised on how best to deal with bears. These were black bears, not usually interested in having an encounter with humans. Students were taught to make noise while walking through the forest (to alert the bear so it could leave) and, in the event of an encounter, to remove the threat to the bear by talking softly and backing away. In later years, we had bear spray as a deterrent, but never had to use it. There was one aggressive bear one season that had no regard for humans. It walked straight through our site while we were all there and took students' daypacks off hooks in an open-sided shelter. It proceeded to spend 90 minutes chewing packs. When we returned the next day, the bear had left a big pile of bear poop in the middle of the site. We never saw the bear again but later learned that it continued to get increasingly aggressive with people elsewhere in the LSCR and had to be put down for safety reasons.

Figure 2.2. Excavating in the Rain. Credit: Nadine Ryan.

buy a high-quality trowel, such as a Marshalltown. Otherwise, they were warned, whatever less costly trowel they purchased or borrowed would break, and they would end up buying a Marshalltown anyway. Some students need to learn by experience, so for a while I kept an exhibit of broken trowels. High-quality rain gear was also strongly recommended. As with the trowels, some needed to learn by experience.

Applying for a spot in the field school was always competitive. Decisions were made by a committee of anthropologists, joined sometimes by a geographer – all understood the nature of archaeological fieldwork. Grades were important, but they did not trump community-mindedness, passion, a sense of adventure, sociability, leadership, volunteerism, and an ability and desire to work collaboratively. As many archaeologists know, students that do well in the classroom do not necessarily do well in the field. Some of the very best of the field school students, including some who have gone on to good careers in archaeology, were "C" students in the classroom.

Some students were creative in their applications. One applicant included photos of her tattoos as proof of her strength to carry heavy buckets of dirt. Of course, there is no correlation between tattoos and strength, but the committee liked her approach. She was accepted. Another student wrote, "I would take a bullet for Bob Muckle. Not in the chest, but in a shoulder or leg for sure." He too was accepted.

Making the Data and Research Meaningful

At the outset, when the project was focusing on merely documenting known settler sites, there was little need to spend much time thinking about how to make the data and the research meaningful. The core plan was to make the results of the fieldwork available to the Metro Vancouver Regional District, for use in its land management plans, and to share the results of our work with the public. As the project continued, however, and especially once the project started excavating Nikkei sites, it became important to figure out how we could make the data meaningful (primarily through lab work) and the research meaningful (by sharing). These topics are covered in Chapter 7.

Of course, two of the most important steps for making data and research meaningful are (i) grounding data collection and research in a meaningful theoretical context and (ii) ensuring that both are conducted ethically – in a way that includes and serves affected communities.

FINDING OUR THEORETICAL COMPASS

It was a challenge for the project director to make the switch from a career in prehistoric archaeology, working mostly in the service of First Nations and a bit in the service of corporations, to an academic project focusing on the early twentieth century and on settler communities, a focus that made public archaeology a major component of the project and running a field school a necessity. This switch required a change not only in methods but also in thinking. It was stressful. There were many sleepless nights and days full of anxiety. But it all worked out.

Eventually the stress and anxiety were relieved, especially once we started discovering and excavating sites associated with Nikkei. These discoveries led to new interests.

Working on the settler sites was interesting and valuable, but we were kind of locked into **culture history**, mostly fine-tuning the local historical record. Working with the Nikkei sites also contributed to culture history, but there was more of an opportunity to practice what is commonly referred to as **processual archaeology**, trying to figure out how the sites and artifacts we were recovering helped broaden our understanding of the culture of Nikkei people who had lived at those sites and of the circumstances that had led them to abandon their homes. It also led to new interest in things commonly associated with **post-processual archaeology**, such as determining the gender and identity of those past residents. It seemed as if, almost overnight, the project shifted from documenting known settler sites to being a significant part of Asian American archaeology and to contributing knowledge about the **Japanese diaspora**, in particular.

As issues in archaeology evolved over the course of the project, so too did the orientation of and thinking informing our work. As archaeologists began increasingly to understand the need to work collaboratively with the descendants of those they study, we started increasingly to reach out to the local Nikkei community. As public archaeology increased its prominence, we increased our outreach. As archaeologists and other heritage professionals started discussing the **curation crisis** (the predicament of too much collected and too few places and people to maintain and care for it), we decided to reduce the collection of artifacts and to return many of those already collected to the field sites. As interests in sustainability increased, the project started doing waste audits, tracking project waste (e.g., broken tools, used flagging tape, packaging) and personal waste (e.g., food waste from students). As studies of sexual harassment and abuse illustrated how extensive it was on archaeological field projects, we adopted an explicit zero tolerance policy.

FINDING OUR ETHICAL COMPASS

There are laws that inform archaeologists of what they must or must not do, and then there are ethics, which inform archaeologists of what they *should* do. Legislation provides a wide swath of options, a range of what archaeologists can do legally. Ethics narrows those options. In British Columbia, for example, the British Columbia Heritage Conservation Act requires archaeologists to obtain a permit from government to undertake fieldwork involving excavation, especially if the site is prehistoric. Obtaining a permit or permission from a local First Nation is not always required, but most archaeologists seek that permission as well because it is widely considered the ethical thing to do.

For many archaeologists, conducting work without the consent of the descendant community is not ethical. As for the Seymour Valley Archaeology Project, it would not have been done without the consent of the local First Nations. If the Nikkei community had not been supportive of the archaeology at the Nikkei sites, that work would not have been undertaken.

Archaeologists are generally considered to have responsibility to (i) descendant communities, (ii) those paying for the research, (iii) the academic community, and (iv) the public. These considerations have guided the project throughout. In practical terms, responsibility to the descendant communities was acknowledged and furthered through numerous interactions with the Nikkei community; we provided site tours, wrote articles for Nikkei newsletters, gave presentations at their community center, and facilitated the transfer of ownership of artifacts from Metro Vancouver to the Nikkei National Museum and Cultural Centre. And what about the project's responsibility to those paying for the research? Even though it might seem as if no one "paid," as there was no transfer of money, both Metro Vancouver and Capilano University offered indirect financial supports. So they received official reports and informal updates regularly. The academic community has been served by more than a dozen presentations on the project's work at academic conferences and by articles in scholarly journals. The public has been served by the many thousands of people reached through outreach, which included presentations, exhibits, on-site experiences, blogging, and participants' wide availability to mainstream media.

There is only one time when the gray area of ethics may have been approached. A senior administrator at the university wanted to visit the excavations and expressed a desire to excavate. At the end of the day prior to the scheduled visit, a student exposed part of a bottle. We did not move the bottle or otherwise alter the context, save for sprinkling a tiny bit of dirt back on top and deciding to let the administrator find it the next morning, which she did.

3

The Archaeology of Settler Sites

This is evidence of a marijuana grow op, Bob.
– Visitor to the site, explaining to the project director
that what the director thought was simply a modern
plastic bottle left by a hiker was much more revealing

INTRODUCTION

This chapter focuses primarily on the project work associated with people living in the study area during the early twentieth century. Also described is a multiuse site (the Hastings/Sparks site), part of which was used for a residence but most of which was likely used as the field offices for a logging company. There is some evidence of Nikkei at the multiuse Hastings/Sparks site, but there is no evidence that the camp was exclusively or primarily a Nikkei site. The Hastings/Sparks site also exhibits recent evidence of its use as a marijuana farm. "Settler," in the context of this project, primarily refers to people of European descent, sometimes alternatively called Euro-Canadians, Canadians, or Whites. The locations of the sites discussed in this chapter, including the Fisherman's Trail sites, the Hastings/Sparks site, and the Martin/McKay site, are identified in Figure 1.2.

There were reports of at least several dozen cabins and houses in the study area, residences dating to the early twentieth century, some legally built and documented but many undocumented and built and lived in without government sanction. The project made no attempt to search for or document most residences. Rather, the places investigated were chosen judgmentally and based largely on their potential for education and resource management: for example, how useful would the sites be in the delivery of public education, and should the sites be protected from future land-altering projects in the LSCR? Of course, there was some research as well, but our primary interest was in the value of the sites for education.

While most of this chapter focuses on the archaeology of settler sites, there is also a concise box feature on the appeal of archaeological fieldwork (Box 3.1).

DOCUMENTING WHAT IS MOSTLY KNOWN: HOMESTEAD SITES ALONG FISHERMAN'S TRAIL

The early field seasons focused almost exclusively on documenting sites in an area along the river known locally as the "homestead area," which, in the early twentieth century, was likely the most densely populated part of the study area (but still, buildings here numbered in the dozens rather than in the hundreds or more). Most of the houses were along "Fisherman's Trail," which runs parallel to the river, and primary access for the residents was via the "Homestead Trail."

Residents generally used the Homestead Trail to get to the closest school or public transit station, which required about an hour's walk. There was a dirt road passing through the homestead area to service the dam several kilometers upstream, but following the road on foot would have required much more travel time than taking the trail. Most residents did not have a car.

The areas receiving the most focus included the Fowler residence; an area of mostly rental cabins known as "The Point"; the location where a yellow cedar log house had been built; and the site of the Barnard residence. We covered the entire length of the homestead area (about

BOX 3.1 THE APPEAL OF ARCHAEOLOGICAL FIELDWORK

One of the objectives of the archaeology field school, and this book, has been to introduce students to the culture of fieldwork. The lifestyle of archaeologists working in the field is usually a far cry from that depicted in popular culture and mainstream media.

Of course, people enjoy archaeology for different reasons, but for many working archaeologists, the appeal of archaeological fieldwork is spending time outdoors, being physically active, traveling and working in remote and sometimes exotic locations, and loving the sense of adventure and discovery. Field archaeologists often like, or are at least comfortable with, a little bit of danger, such as working among bears and rattlesnakes. Many like the image of archaeology depicted in popular culture, even though they know it isn't real. There is also the sociability factor (being around like-minded people 24/7) and being able to wear comfortable clothes. For some, it is more about being in an unstructured work environment (as compared to an office, for example) or having necessities provided (such as food and accommodation). Some like the precarious nature of field archaeology, its unexpectedness; they enjoy having the ability to pick up work on a project-by-project basis.

Those who work on a project-by-project basis, often for multiple companies, are sometimes called **shovelbums**. Some like constant fieldwork, while others choose to balance fieldwork with other archaeology-related work, such as classifying and analyzing artifacts and other recovered remains in a lab, writing reports and doing other office work, and teaching.

1 km) on foot, but except for digging a few test pits in our search for the Barnard residence, we restricted our investigation to a surface survey.

Fisherman's Trail and the Homestead Trail remain in use today and are very popular with visitors to the LSCR, both pedestrians and cyclists. Evidence of some historic activities along the Homestead Trail is visible, but many people are oblivious. Most of the evidence is hidden, close to but off the trail.

Figure 3.1 shows field school students conducting an archaeological survey (looking for archaeological sites) between Fisherman's Trail and the Seymour River. They follow compass bearings and are closely spaced to ensure full visual coverage of the ground surface.

Comments from Some Early Residents

Those doing historical archaeology sometimes have the benefit of spending time with people who have firsthand knowledge of the area and time period being studied. Such was the case with this project. I was able to spend time with three of the early residents of the area: Flynn Fowler, who lived in the area from 1928 to 1950; George Barnard, who lived in the area from 1920 to about 1937; and Carl Sparks, who lived in the area in the 1930s and early 1940s. I had several hours of conversation with these three, both individually and in combination, during the early years of the project.

Knowing where to look for trash would presumably help us locate artifacts, so Flynn Fowler and George Barnard were each asked, "What did your family do with the trash?" The Fowler's property included 800 feet of riverfront, and without hesitation, Flynn replied that it was his job to get rid of the trash – "It all went in the river," he said. George's family lived in a house on approximately five acres, but with no direct river access. The Barnards dug a deep hole into which they tossed their trash.

The Fowlers were the last residents to live in the study area, and Flynn Fowler was able to recall the final destruction of area properties. He recalled local houses being deliberately burned by the Greater Vancouver Water District. He remembers seeing the flames shooting out of the Barnard house. He also recalls the deliberate demolition of other built structures and their contents, as the Greater Vancouver Water District began limiting public access. Buildings and other materials were being tossed into the river or left along the riverbank.

These conversations explained some of our findings, or rather lack of findings. We had done intensive surface surveys of George Barnard's property, finding nothing. Similarly, while some features of the cabins and houses along the river were identified **in situ** (e.g., crumbled bricks

Figure 3.1. Looking for Sites along Fisherman's Trail. Credit: R. Muckle.

and mortar from chimneys), 90 per cent of the artifacts we discovered were close to or within the river embankment.

George Barnard, Flynn Fowler, and Carl Sparks had many good memories, recalling, for example, racing their sleds in winter, and bikes the rest of the year, down the steep Homestead Trail, resulting one time in George missing a turn and knocking himself unconscious. People from elsewhere in Metro Vancouver occasionally visited the area by vehicle throughout the summer and on weekends the rest of the year. George remembers his mom shooting the tires out of a car transporting people intent on raiding her garden.

The Fowlers and Barnards had no electricity or telephones. The Barnards had no plumbing and got their water from a small creek at the back of their property. The Fowlers tapped into the water line running from Seymour Lake past their property.

The Fowler Property

The Fowler property is among the most archaeologically visible sites in the LSCR. According to Flynn Fowler, the family owned 800 feet of river frontage between Fisherman's Trail and the river, a little bit less than an acre in total. Along Fisherman's Trail today can be seen two old wooden arches, with two upright posts and another laid horizontally over the others. One arch led to the main entrance of the house, and the other led from the path to the yard, which included a barn and garden. Dating close to a century in age, the arches are not very stable now, but they are clearly distinguishable. The property is currently heavily vegetated. A short walk through one of the arches leads to the concrete foundation of the Fowler residence. Few artifacts have been recorded here. One that was recorded – a 1923 dime.

Besides speaking with Flynn Fowler, project investigators surveyed the Fowler homestead, documenting its features. Doing so required them to learn survey techniques and how to document findings. Students followed transects running east to west through the property, which considering the thick vegetation was often difficult. In addition to the archways and concrete foundation, students were able to identify several wooden fence posts on their way to slowly becoming indistinguishable from nature.

There were few significant or interesting artifacts found on the Fowler property. This may be explained in several ways. As Flynn described, when the Greater Vancouver Water District evicted families, the houses and contents were burned and remains moved into the river. Other explanations might include the Fowlers taking most things with them; the several decades of forest growth and soil development burying what was left behind; and the looting of the site along this popular trail since the reopening of the LSCR in 1987.

The Point

One section of the homestead area is known locally as "The Point"; presumably, its name is derived from the triangular shape of land that marks its boundaries, like a point jutting into the river. During the early twentieth century, this area included several rental cabins and one permanent house that also doubled, for a time, as a store. It was apparently a particularly popular spot for recreation in the summers, and in addition to the cabins, there were also spots for tenting. The river took some turns in this area, creating pools, which were good for swimming. As with all other residential structures in the area, the cabins and house/store were all deliberately destroyed in the 1940s and early 1950s. The area is now covered in thick vegetation.

As with the Fowler property, we used this area for teaching and learning field survey techniques. The most obvious feature is a large fireplace constructed of cobbles, bricks, and mortar (Figure 3.2). It is only about 5 meters off Fisherman's Trail, but relatively few people who walk or bike the trail are aware of it, such is the density of surrounding vegetation. According to Flynn Fowler, this fireplace was inside one of the rental cabins. It remains a mystery why this fireplace was left standing when all the fireplaces and chimneys in the entire study area, including the several others in the immediate area of The Point, were not. It may be that those doing the demolition just never finished the job or saw the beauty in it and decided to leave it. We were able to identify several other residential structures by chimney debris or other rock features, including a small rock wall, presumably part of a garden.

Most of the artifacts discovered in this area would have been recognized as trash, including many broken bottles. One bottle we found was complete and sealed, half full of an amber liquid. It was probably ground water that had seeped into the bottle over the past several decades, but it was great for public presentations and exhibits. People

Figure 3.2. Fireplace in the Forest. Credit: R. Muckle.

would ask, "What's in the bottle?" "Could be brandy," I'd reply, "but in reality, it's probably groundwater." "Why not open it and find out?" they'd ask. And to that, I would respond, "I'd rather not know. If it's just groundwater, nobody would care, and fewer people would engage with the exhibit."

We also found some small fragments of an old vinyl record. The label was unreadable, but we could see its bluish color. When we combined that evidence with some imprints of numbers in the vinyl, we were able to conclude that the record was "Broken Heart Polka," recorded by

Romy Gosz and his Orchestra for Decca in 1939. One of the students who discovered the vinyl fragments, Suzannah Forbes, is the daughter of well-known local musician Roy Forbes (formerly known as Bim). It was Roy who determined the details of the recording.

The Log House

We heard that a yellow cedar log house had been built in the early twentieth century along the river, but we found no visible remains of this house in the study area. Yellow cedar was and remains a highly valued timber, and therefore it was not common to build houses with it. Most houses in the region were constructed of other, less costly, kinds of cedar. The origins of the house are unclear, but it appears to have been built around 1900 and used mostly as a residence for senior employees of the Greater Vancouver Water District. Carl Sparks lived in the house in the early 1940s while his father was an employee. Although all other built structures in the area were burned or otherwise demolished, permission was granted in the late 1940s to dismantle the house and reassemble it elsewhere in North Vancouver, where it remains today.

Because there is so much local interest in the property, despite knowing no remains of the house would be found, we decided to see what else we might find. So we invited Carl Sparks to help us search for the house's location, several decades after he had lived there as a child. He recalled the property had a "lily pond" constructed of stone and concrete about 3 meters (10 feet) in diameter and 1 meter (3 feet) high. As elsewhere in the homestead area, vegetation was thick, but we persisted. It took a few students working a few days, but eventually they were able to locate the lily pond, as described by Carl. No other remains were visible.

The Barnard Residence

George Barnard provided an oral history of the homestead area, and we wanted to find some physical evidence of his time living in the region. We were stifled though. We did an intensive surface survey where he had lived but did not find a single feature or artifact. We also dug test pits near the Barnard residence, the only places in the homestead area where we looked subsurface, but they were all **sterile**.

Other Areas of Interest in the Homestead Area

Other areas of interest in the homestead area included a tunnel through solid rock for a wooden water pipe. A large water pipe constructed of wooden planks bound with metal straps once carried water alongside Fisherman's Trail, taking the water from the reservoir. It was presumably easier to blast a tunnel than bend a wooden pipeline, so the tunnel was constructed. The tunnel is about 30 meters (100 feet) long, the pipe long gone. About 200 of the 217 field school students have run or walked through the tunnel, for no reason other than it was a fun thing to do.

Unexpectedly, while following up on a rumor of possible house remains, we discovered a discrete trash dump. It appears to be a combination of an unsanctioned trash dump from the early twentieth century and a site with modern trash, including several small empty propane canisters, contemporary empty beer cans, and one almost-new Nike sneaker. We are interpreting the modern refuse as being left by homeless people living in the forest.

Another anomaly is clamshells on and close to the Homestead Trail. It was initially thought that the shells might have been used to stabilize the trail (shells are used widely as a road-building material). One enterprising student wasn't satisfied though, so she continued to search and found many more shells on the steep hillside beside the trail. The origin and context of these shells remains a mystery. At the top of the hillside, where we found the shells, is currently located a works yard for the LSCR, and there are also a few lots that once had houses on them. The shells may have once been stored in the works yard, but none of the consulted LSCR staff had any recollection of shells being there or of them being used in any manner. An alternative is that the shells were part of tossed, decades-old household trash from one of the residences.

AN ACCIDENTAL DISCOVERY OF AN EARLY RESIDENCE – THE MARTIN/MCKAY SITE

There is a gate to prevent vehicle access into the LSCR, with a staff person there to let authorized people through, including the project director (me). Often, the person on the gate and I would have a brief chat, both when I entered and left the reserve. One day when I was leaving, the operator of the gate indicated that someone had reported a potential new site, and that another staff person could show it to me now. I parked my truck.

It was only a few hundred meters from the gate, and not far off a service road. Earlier in the day, someone was walking through the forest (purpose unknown) and almost fell down a small shaft leading to a deep pit of water hidden by the forest. The adventure was reported to the staff at the gate.

It took only minutes to decide to do some further investigating. The shaft that the person almost fell down was constructed of wood planks leading to an expanded underground water reservoir. It was easy to understand how the person had not seen it. The area was heavily covered with vegetation. Despite the vegetation, beyond the water reservoir, the project director was able to observe dozens of artifacts (mostly broken dishes and bottles) and a cluster of bricks and mortar, presumably remnants of a chimney.

A historic land title search indicated that the site was occupied from 1911 to 1942 by Ella Martin and from 1942 to 1946 by Clara Belle McKay and Marjorie Dorothy McKay, before being purchased and then destroyed by the Greater Vancouver Water District.

The top opening of the water reservoir was built with cedar planks, measuring 76 cm (2'6") square going straight down for 91 cm (3 feet). At the 91 cm below-surface mark, the reservoir expanded several meters in each direction and reached a depth of 2.7 meters (9'6"), measured with a stadia rod. The walls of the expanded portion were primarily natural clay soils. One passionate-for-scuba student pleaded to dive in the reservoir. It was too risky though. The risk outweighed the possible reward. There was probably nothing to see. The water was clear. We could see to the bottom already.

A flat cleared area at the rear of the property may have been part of the Lillooet Trail. At least one map shows the Lillooet Trail here. Hundreds of artifacts were visible on the surface, mostly broken dishes, bottles, and jars. Excavations revealed many more household items, including more dishes, more bottles, buttons, gloves, boots, a flashlight, and a pocketknife. We also discovered several coins – dating to 1937, 1941, and 1942 – and several hundred nails, presumably from house construction.

Revisiting the site in 2019, I observed some small plastic pots, which may have been used for growing marijuana. I also observed a recently constructed shelter made from tree branches. Given the location, we presumed this was a temporary shelter built by one or more homeless people.

LOOKING WHERE WE SHOULDN'T AND FINDING THE HASTINGS/SPARKS SITE

Occasionally, LSCR staff would ask if we could try to locate particular sites, mostly in areas that had been rumored to have remains but were never properly documented. One field season, a supervisor asked if we could try to find and document the location of a cabin that was once lived in by the family of Carl Sparks in the early twentieth century. We had an approximate location, narrowing it down as being somewhere along a strip of now heavily vegetated land approximately 1 km in length between the riverbank and a service road. People had looked before but couldn't find it.

As we were getting ready to do the survey, I was approached by some LSCR staff to discuss some unrelated things. I had already given the crew background on the potential Sparks site and directions as to the techniques to use there (i.e., surveying via transects, walking through the dense brush and trees between and parallel to the riverbank and old access road), so I was confident in setting them on their way, with notice that I would catch up in about 10 to 15 minutes.

As I was walking the trail toward where I expected the students to be, I heard some rustling in the bushes to the east of me, up an embankment in the forest. The students were supposed to be to the west, between the trail and the river. At first, I thought it was probably a bear, but I soon heard voices. "Who is up there?" I called. A student answered and gave two names, to which I replied, "What are you doing up there? You are supposed to be surveying on the other side of the trail." The student responded, "I think you will want to see this."

I scrambled up the embankment, and the students showed me some scattered remains of a metal stove and bed. The three of us spent about another 15 minutes looking around and found several indications of a camp of some sort, as identified from evidence of multiple stoves. At about the 10-minute mark, I discovered a Japanese rice bowl in a small creek running through the site. (This would be the third site with evidence of a Nikkei presence in the valley.) Considering that the site was easily accessed (it took only about 40 minutes each way to walk the trail to it, and you could get close with a vehicle for transporting equipment and supplies) and that it provided evidence of a temporary logging camp, was unknown in the local community, and had indications of Nikkei, I decided this would be a good place to document and excavate.

There was a creek running through the central portion of the site. A large clear plastic beverage bottle could be seen in the embankment a few meters from where we used a piece of wood to create a bridge over the creek. I had pointed it out to all the students and visitors to the site as an example of trash left by recent hikers or bikers. This site, although easily accessible to its former occupants, was now off the beaten path, requiring a scramble up an embankment or about a 100-meter walk through dense vegetation from a mountain bike trail, but finding modern trash there was not totally unexpected.

Further surface surveying revealed a concrete foundation for a small building. Consultation with LSCR staff led to recollections that a logging company – the Hastings Company – was known to have a field office somewhere in the vicinity in the early twentieth century, but the precise location was unknown. Given that the trail was an access road in the early twentieth century, this made sense. It still didn't explain the evidence of several cabins having been there or the artifacts associated with Nikkei, though.

While I was scrambling through the bush on that initial day of discovery with two students on the east side of the trail, the rest of the students ultimately did discover evidence related to the cabin we were originally looking for. The trail had simply bisected the site. We named the site the Hastings/Sparks site to reflect its two principal users: the Hastings Company and later the Sparks family.

The original cabin was reported to have been occupied by the Sparks family in the 1930s, the same family that occupied the yellow cedar log house in the homestead area during the early 1940s. I invited Carl Sparks to come have a look. He hadn't been to the site in close to 70 years but was able to confirm that the site we discovered was indeed his old residence. Carl related that his family moved onto the property in the 1930s. He understood that they were moving onto a property where a logging company had some operations (but not a camp) with several buildings, one of which they converted to a house.

When we showed Carl the evidence of the camp across the trail, he was shocked. He had no recollection of this part of the site whatsoever, which would have almost literally been in his backyard. Such is the nature of abandonment and forest growth in the study area; most surface evidence is quickly covered within a few years.

Excavations have led us to believe that the part of the site west of the trail, where the Sparks family lived in the 1930s, has been relatively undisturbed. We found a few concrete foundations and scattered household trash, likely associated with the Sparks family.

The part of the site east of the trail up an embankment was a bit more complicated. We chose an area to start our excavations based on the evidence: at the bottom of a slope, some surface trash suggested that location as a **midden**. This is an example of **judgmental sampling** (archaeological sampling that is directed by the archaeologist's purpose, expertise, or guess). It contrasts with **nonjudgmental sampling**, which uses some form of random selection. It became apparent that that the midden was probably created by different sets of people at different times.

Excavations led to recording hundreds of artifacts, including parts of metal cook stoves, bed frames, saw blades, many beer and pharmaceutical bottles, and broken dishes, including those of Japanese origins.

Based on the limited excavations at the site (one field season only), we established a tentative life history of the site. It is likely that sometime in the late 1800s or early 1900s, there was a logging camp here. This explains the indications of several cabins (based on stoves and beds) and many of the bottles and dishes, including those of Japanese origin. The site was probably in use as a camp for only a few years. A few years or more after the logging camp was abandoned, in the early years of the twentieth century, the Hastings Company built some field offices here. The field offices were abandoned, probably in the early or mid-1920s, and forest regrowth quickly covered much evidence of the eastern portion of the site, so much so that when the Sparks family lived in the western portion of the site from 1938 to 1940, its members were not even aware of the evidence of settlement in the eastern portion (at least Carl wasn't). After several more decades had passed, sometime in the late years of the twentieth century or the early years of the twenty-first century, some people had used the eastern portion of the site for a small-scale marijuana farm. Given that the site would take physical exertion to reach and had very basic technology, the farmers were probably teenagers or young adults. The site was about 100 meters off a popular mountain bike trail. It is conceivable that this bike trail was the primary access for those cultivating the marijuana.

During excavations one day, a supervisor in the LSCR came for a tour. I walked him through the site. When he spotted the clear plastic bottle in the creek, he enlightened me. Walking the few meters to the bottle in the embankment and stooping to pick it up, he said, "This is evidence of a marijuana grow op Bob." The bottom of the bottle had been cut off and the rest of the bottle had a few dozen small perforations drilled into it, all perfectly round. "This is part of an irrigation system. Each of these perforations would have had a plastic tube running from it to elsewhere on the site. The bottle would have been anchored in the creek with the open end collecting water, which was redistributed by the tubing." I felt both silly (for previously not even bothering to look closely at the bottle) and informed.

The next day while the students were excavating, I was scouring the site looking for more evidence of a marijuana grow op. I discovered a small bit of a wool sock poking through the ground surface. I thought, "among the students, who might be most likely to know the intricacies of an outdoor marijuana grow op?" I called the student over and asked him if he could see any connection between this piece of sock and a grow op. Without hesitation, the student replied, "Do you remember how cold the days were when we got here, but still, lots of sun? It was still too cold for seeds to grow but there was plenty of sunlight. Wrapping the seedlings in socks protected them from cold while taking advantage of the sun. They only would have needed the socks early in spring." We subsequently found more perforated plastic bottles near the creek.

ASSESSING THE SIGNIFICANCE OF THE SETTLER SITES

Overall, the settler sites are considered to have moderate to high public significance but low scientific significance, historic significance, ethnic significance, and economic significance.

The Fowler site is evaluated as having moderate to high public significance primarily on the basis of its ease of access – it's alongside a popular recreation trail – and its highly visible and interpretable features, such as the wooden arches and concrete foundation.

The fireplace at The Point is similarly evaluated as having moderate to high public significance based on its high archaeological visibility and ease of access.

The Martin/McKay site had high public significance insofar as it provided opportunity to participate in excavations. Without active excavations, though, the significance is only moderate. Compared to the other settler sites, this site was more difficult to access and its archaeological visibility was low.

The Hastings/Sparks site is evaluated as having moderate to low scientific significance. There may be some research value in continued excavations, but there is low public, ethnic, historic, or economic significance. The site is more difficult for the public to reach, and there are few visible remnants of its occupation.

PUBLIC ARCHAEOLOGY WITH THE SETTLER SITES AND ARTIFACTS

The settler sites were, overall, fantastic for public education. Many groups, including K–12 classes, were given tours of the homestead area in which they learned about both archaeology field methods and local history. Participants also got the opportunity to run through the old water pipe tunnel.

The Martin/McKay site was fantastic for both public education and excavation. It was easily accessed and had high archaeological visibility, so we could have weekends during which the public was invited to participate in excavations, in disturbed areas likely to have artifacts and under the close supervision of the project director and students.

There were many exhibits of artifacts throughout the project years, and visitors to the exhibits were generally most interested in the artifacts associated with the settler sites, presumably because they were settlers themselves and could identify with the artifacts. Favorites included a glass Orange Crush bottle from the 1930s, a ceramic ginger beer bottle, and the sealed bottle containing an amber liquid. There was little interest in anything metal or in the broken dishes from the settler sites. It was clearly bottles that people liked to see and touch. And hundreds, perhaps thousands, did.

4

A Logging Camp at Suicide Creek

Project Director: I'm looking for something a bit more challenging and out of public view, perhaps a logging camp.
Eric Crossin, retired forester: I know of such a place. Let me
show you.
– Conversation between the project director and Eric
Crossin, who had spent thousands of hours
in the LSCR mapping old logging roads

INTRODUCTION

When first hearing of the Suicide Creek site, people often ask about the name. "What's the story on the name?" is a common question. We gave it the name because of its proximity to a known creek, identified on many maps as "Suicide Creek." Some maps also show a feature linked to the creek identified as "Suicide Bluffs." One can guess that perhaps the bluffs and creek were named because of the real or imagined potential that someone could commit suicide by jumping off the bluffs, but we don't know. As with many sites, names are sometimes used by archaeologists without much thought beyond temporary convenience.

We just started to refer to the site by this name to distinguish it from the other sites in the region we were also investigating at the time, and it stuck. We didn't really know what was there, beyond scattered evidence of a logging camp, so we just used its location as the name.

Unknown to us at the time of the decision to work here, this site was established and used for a few years around 1920 as a Nikkei logging camp.

After concentrating for a few years almost exclusively on the settler sites, especially those in the homestead area, I wanted something a bit more challenging, and also out of public view. Additionally, the public education and resource management aims for those areas were played out, so it was prudent to start looking elsewhere, especially as those two aims were among our principal motivating interests. We continued working at the settler sites throughout the project, but our primary attention turned to sites associated with Nikkei and logging, beginning with the Suicide Creek site.

This chapter describes the initial discovery and assessment of the site, as well as the field methods we used there. It also provides an overview of the site's features and artifacts, of its significance, and of the public education associated with it.

DISCOVERY AND INITIAL ASSESSMENT

As alluded to in the epigraph to this chapter, we were looking for somewhere new to investigate and excavate. Because I was still fairly new to doing historical archaeology (this was before discovering and working at the Hastings/Sparks site discussed in Chapter 3), I wanted the new site to be out of view of the public. I didn't want the distraction of the public while I was pretty much learning the ins and outs of excavating historic period sites. I also knew that while the archaeology of settler sites was common, the archaeology of logging camps was not. I thought we could offer some value to archaeology there, working on the archaeology of logging camps.

Eric showed me the site. It was perfect. To reach it required a drive of several kilometers on access roads, a hike of a few hundred meters along an overgrown search and rescue trail, and then about 30 meters of bushwhacking. The site was heavily overgrown, with no standing structures. There were, however, some visible cedar planking and scatterings of artifacts easy to associate with a camp, including a metal wash basin, a few broken bottles, bits of a saw blade, and several cans that were likely indicative of a larger midden below.

It would have been about a two-hour walk each way for students, but fortunately the LSCR staff volunteered to transport students to the trailhead of the search and rescue trail via a small bus on a daily basis. This made it easy to decide to do some archaeology here.

The initial assessment we made, based on the surface evidence, was that this was almost certainly a relatively small early twentieth century logging camp. Further, there was no evidence of disturbance since it was abandoned close to a century earlier (i.e., it had excellent **site integrity**). There was no evidence of digging, for example, no evidence of a pathway leading directly to or from the site, and no accumulation of artifacts in a single place, which for some reason is a common activity of non-archaeologists when they find a site – collecting surface artifacts and leaving them in one place. Of course, one never knows what pothunters may have collected from the surface, but the location of the site in a fairly remote area and an examination of the surface suggested little or no disturbance since the loggers left the camp, except for the burning of the camp. Whether the camp was burned deliberately or by design is unknown. We know fires were not uncommon in the study area throughout the early twentieth century, started naturally by lightning strikes or by accident, perhaps by oil lanterns being knocked over, or deliberately by government officials, who burned down structures to prevent people living in them.

SURVEY AND EXCAVATION STRATEGIES

Thinking about excavating a historic period site was initially stressful and anxiety ridden. I wanted to make sure I got it right. I was new to historical archaeology and didn't want to mess it up. One of the things about field archaeology is that it isn't very forgiving. By its very nature, archaeology is destructive. We destroy as we excavate. There are no second chances.

Knowing we were going to do extensive work at the site, I realized it was necessary to create a **site datum**, a point to which all measurements could be tied. We created the site datum point by driving a 4-foot piece of **rebar** vertically into the ground, so that only the tip was at the surface, which we marked with flagging tape. We used rebar because it is metal, giving it a sense of permanence and making it easy to relocate with a metal detector in future.

Our first task was to survey the area around the site. We did this to establish the site boundaries. We did intensive surveying in transects a few meters apart for a few hundred meters in each direction, which was often difficult considering the thick vegetation and very challenging and unstable terrain in much of the area. We were, however, able to distinguish clear boundaries. We were also able to identify several different **cedar plank roads** (with most planks removed) leading to and from the site. As described elsewhere, cedar plank roads would have been used to haul sleds of **shingle bolts**.

Figure 4.1 pictures field school students walking through the central portion of the site, a Nikkei (Japanese Canadian) logging camp operational for a few years in the early 1920s. Floorboards of the mess hall are to the left of the students.

We also used a metal detector in selected areas when trying to determine the boundaries of the site. The metal detector led to the discovery of a water pipe running from an unnamed creek for about 100 meters to the site, ending close to the location of the kitchen area. The pipe was subsurface, but on average only a few centimeters below ground. We surmised that the pipe originally may have laid on the ground surface, on a steep slope from the water source's location to the site. It may have subsequently been buried by natural processes. We located about 50 per cent of the pipe, surmising that the missing sections either were taken when the loggers abandoned the camp or simply became disconnected through time and rolled down the hillside into the creek. We did not look intensively for the missing pieces. It was important that we found the pipe bringing water to the site but searching for the missing pieces wasn't deemed to be a good use of our time. At the source (where the pipe was placed in the creek), the pipe had a 3/4 inch diameter. At its termination in the camp, the diameter was 1/2 inch.

Surveying included mapping the entire surface of the site. We began by placing a 10-meter by 10-meter grid over the entire site but then reduced the grid size when excavations had the potential to get complex. For example, on the periphery of the site, where there was little

Figure 4.1. Walking through the Suicide Creek Site. Credit: M. Galvani.

or no evidence of cultural remains, we kept with the 10 by 10 meter grid, plotting in, for example, large trees. The core area of the site we initially mapped mostly in 5 by 5 meter grids to capture the features. The surfaces of the areas chosen for excavating in 2-meter by 2-meter sections were also mapped to scale.

Excavating was done in 2-meter by 2-meter units, by trowel and sifting through 6 mm mesh screens. We excavated to 5 or 10 cm arbitrary levels of depth. We also took the opportunity to look in the roots of recently fallen trees. Returning to the site one Monday after a particularly stormy weekend, we noticed one tree had uprooted during the storm. Entangled in the roots was a clearly visible Japanese rice bowl.

One of the primary objectives of excavations at this site was to determine the camp layout, such as the location of one or more bunkhouses, a midden, and a kitchen and eating area. We didn't really know what to expect. There is much documentary evidence of how the large logging camps in the Pacific Northwest were constructed but little in the way of how the small camps were built. A review of literature on logging operations showed that some small camps were fairly structured, with buildings aligned, for example, while photos of others showed build-ings located in an almost chaotic manner.

Areas chosen for excavation were chosen judgmentally, in other words, after an evaluation based on surface indications of potential features, such as evidence of cedar planks or dense concentrations of artifacts.

Excavations at the Suicide Creek site occurred over parts of five field seasons. In total, about 15 per cent of the site was excavated, and 95 per cent of the artifacts were recovered subsurface.

THE FEATURES AT SUICIDE CREEK

We were able to identify several distinct features, including the locations of a bunkhouse, a cooking and mess hall area, a trash midden, a workshop that focused on blacksmithing and farrier (horse-related) work, and a workshop that focused on logging-related tools. Each of these features was identified based on clusters of artifacts, such as heating stoves, fragments of work boots, and door hardware, which we used to locate the bunk-house. The bunkhouse was also identifiable by the charred floorboards. Similarly, the cookhouse and mess hall structure was identified by a large cookstove, clusters of cooking and serving artifacts, charred floorboards, and its close proximity to the midden, which was comprised primarily of refuse related to consumption (e.g., food cans, bottles, and jars).

Figure 4.2 illustrates the boundaries of the site, as well as the size and locations of the features. Figure 4.3 is a sketch reconstructing what a portion of the site likely looked like while in use, about 1920.

THE ARTIFACTS AT SUICIDE CREEK

We recorded 517 artifacts from the Suicide Creek site. We calculated the minimum number of each class of artifact collected. Overall, the assemblage of artifacts recovered at this site represents a minimum of 78 bottles (alcohol, pharmaceutical, and ink), 18 Japanese bowls and plates, 62 cans (food, tobacco, and boot polish), and 105 industrial ar-tifacts (saw blades; files; peaveys, which are hand tools for moving logs; and shoes for workhorses).

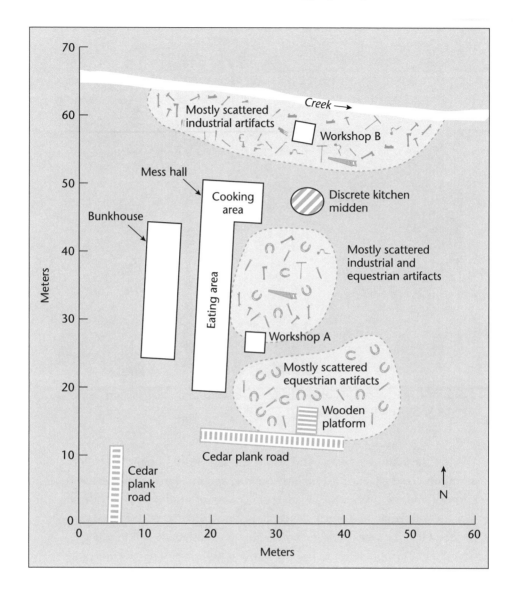

Figure 4.2. Map of the Suicide Creek Site.

Figure 4.3. Reconstruction Drawing of the Suicide Creek Logging Camp, circa 1920. Credit: K. Cook.

All the tableware (plates and bowls) was Japanese in origin; no cutlery was observed except for one large serving spoon. Many of the pharmaceutical bottles were also Japanese, and alcohol bottles included those from both Japan and North America. Japanese alcohol bottles once contained beer or sake. Cans included those for food, boot polish, tobacco, and talc. Personal items were rare, but we did recover a metal comb and a single piece of costume jewelry, with fake diamonds. We know it is costume jewelry because one of the students took it to a jeweler to make sure.

There were many horse-related artifacts found, which makes sense considering that teams of horses are known to have been in wide use in the logging industry in the valley in the early decades of the twentieth century. We recovered 51 large horseshoes. According to the multiple students familiar with horses, the horseshoes were likely for **Percherons**, a breed of **draft horse**. Consultations with farriers about our discoveries confirmed this opinion. We also recovered a harness, pieces of a hame (a curved support attached to the collar of a draft horse), multiple buckles, and a bit – all also likely for Percherons.

Other assorted artifacts include pieces of leather work boots, parts of stoves (both a heating stove and a cookstove), lantern glass, and window glass. One coin was found, within the area of the bunkhouse. It is an 1899 Canadian dime. We figure it fell through the floorboards.

One season when the project returned to the site for further work, we could not relocate the site datum, which seemed odd. We had a metal detector, which should have made it easy but didn't. I got students busy with other tasks while I continued to search for the datum. Evidently, someone had removed it, which was a very unethical thing to do (see Box 4.1).

ON THE PRESENCE OF NIKKEI AT SUICIDE CREEK

There was no surface evidence of Nikkei at Suicide Creek. Neither was there any documentary evidence that there would be a Nikkei logging camp, at least in the initial years of our work at the site. There were a few vague mentions of Nikkei logging in the valley but no specifics about where a camp might be. Likewise, documentary research showed no suggestion of any logging company owning the property or seeking permission to log the area.

It was only when we started excavating and we started finding multiple Japanese dishes and bottles with Japanese writing that we realized that the camp was occupied by Nikkei.

Over the course of the project, a periodical of the Archaeological Society of British Columbia titled *The Midden* published several short reports on the project, usually summarizing the field season. Following the initial report on excavations at the Suicide Creek site, a reader suggested the site might have been a camp established by a prominent Nikkei businessman, Eikichi Kagetsu. The reader had done some historical research on him for an unrelated project and recalled that he likely had done some work in the Seymour Valley at some point. With this lead, I was able to track down and contact Tadashi (Jack) Kagetsu, the son of Eikichi Kagetsu. Tadashi Kagetsu was retired, living in New York, and writing a biography of his father. Eventually the biography was published posthumously (Kagetsu 2017).

In the early years of the project, Tadashi Kagetsu was an enormous help with the research. He freely shared the research he had done

BOX 4.1 FIELDWORK ETHICS

Following a hiatus of a few seasons during which we did not work at the Suicide Creek site, we returned there for some further work. The first task was to relocate the site datum, a 4-foot piece of rebar placed vertically. Initially it couldn't be relocated, even with the use of a metal detector. This was disturbing. We knew where the site datum should have been, and it was not visible to any member of the public who might have come across the site.

We searched a much broader area and eventually found the rebar. It was several meters away, placed horizontally and covered by a few centimeters of soil. This was odd, very odd. But it got worse. Scraping more soil we recovered several flakes of obsidian, a kind of stone commonly used for making stone tools but one that does not occur naturally in the study area. Further, a few of the flakes showed evidence of being retouched, with the edges being sharpened for use as a tool. This was crazy. We had worked at the site for multiple previous field seasons and were confident that there were no prehistoric artifacts to be found, but here was a cache of obsidian artifacts. It was both puzzling and disturbing. Through further excavation around the lithic flakes, we found several recent coins (all from the previous 10 years) mixed with the flakes and the relocated rebar we had used as a site datum. The coins were a signal to whomever found the cache of flakes that it was a hoax – someone had planted the obsidian flakes. To make sure we didn't take the find seriously, the hoaxer had put in the coins, so we would know it was fake, and presumably had moved the site datum rebar, knowing we would look for it.

Who moved the datum and planted the artifacts? That remains a mystery. I can't imagine it was one of the 100 or more field school students who worked at the site. They all are advised about the importance of site integrity. It may have been one of the many visitors to the site, who knew the location of the site datum. Whoever did it had knowledge of archaeology.

Planting artifacts is a clear violation of archaeological ethics.

Ethics are important in field archaeology. All major associations of archaeologists have codes of ethics indicating how archaeologists should conduct themselves. In short, most archaeologists recognize they have responsibilities to other archaeologists, the organizations that fund their projects, the descendant community or communities, and the public.

Widely shared ethics of field archaeology further include leaving the site as close to the condition as it was in when you came across it, which includes **backfilling** the excavation units. In the Seymour Valley Archaeology Project, we also did some replanting of small trees and shrubs.

The codes of ethics of many associations of archaeologists also include statements about the responsibilities of project leaders to ensure an equitable and safe working environment. This includes taking steps to secure participants' physical safety, such as not putting students or crew members at risk of physical danger. Ethical guidelines are also directed at ensuring that archaeological workers face no prejudice based on "ableism" (e.g., lack of accessibility), ethnicity, gender, or religion and that they are free from sexual harassment and abuse, in other words, that they have personal as well as physical safety.

himself using his father's personal and business records as well as the research he had contracted professional historians to do. Tadashi Kagetsu indicated that his father had established and operated two Nikkei logging camps in the valley. He mentioned there was probably a camp near Lot 922 and then another in an undetermined part of the valley. It was a year after our initial discussions that we discovered the camp near Lot 922 (the McKenzie Creek site, discussed in Chapters 5 and 6). The Suicide Creek site, we surmised, was probably the other camp.

There was some media attention following the discovery of the Suicide Creek site, because of our findings related to the Nikkei presence there. It was an early lesson about being careful with journalists. Almost all media attention associated with the project has been positive, but there was a situation in the early years that was a bit disturbing. A journalist associated with a major media outlet spent a day at the site with me. The journalist asked for the contact information of Tadashi Kagetsu, and I responded that he had very clearly told me that while he was happy to discuss things with me, he had no interest whatsoever in talking with the media, and I wanted to respect that. The journalist told me that she and her crew were very interested in the Nikkei presence in the valley during the early twentieth century and were going to do more research on the topic themselves, promising to contact Tadashi Kagetsu only to share discoveries and not to ask him questions or to request that he share his own research.

I was dismayed a few months later when Tadashi contacted me to let me know that the journalist had contacted him with questions, reminding me about his wishes. It is with immense gratitude that I report that Tadashi Kagetsu continued to correspond with me. Much of what we know or surmise about the Suicide Creek and McKenzie Creek sites are because of the graciousness of Tadashi Kagetsu.

ASSESSING THE SIGNIFICANCE OF THE SUICIDE CREEK SITE

Overall, the Suicide Creek site is assessed as having moderate to high significance.

Regarding scientific significance, the assessment is moderate to high. This is based largely on the integrity of the deposit, although that integrity has been compromised somewhat by some unethical behavior (i.e., the planting of artifacts, as described in Box 4.1). It was also compromised by the Seymour Valley Archaeology Project undertaking excavations, disturbing the site in that process. Its significance lies in being associated with logging and Nikkei, neither of which has received much attention by archaeologists in western Canada.

Its ethnic significance is assessed as being high. This assessment is based primarily on the importance of this site for the Nikkei community in Canada. It is one of only a handful of Nikkei sites excavated in the country, and one of only two associated with Nikkei logging (the other being the McKenzie Creek site). Artifacts from the Suicide Creek site are on exhibit at the Nikkei National Museum and Cultural Centre.

The site's public significance is assessed as being moderate to low. While excavations were ongoing, it had a higher rating because archaeologists were on site to interpret and supervise. The remoteness of the site's location, including the need to hike little-used trails and difficult trails to get to it, is also considered in this low assessment.

The economic significance of this site is nonexistent.

PUBLIC ARCHAEOLOGY AND THE SUICIDE CREEK SITE

During the seasons of excavation at the site, there was considerable public programming.

We had several K–12 school groups spend a day with us, learning about the process of archaeology and helping to record, map, and draw, but without participating in excavation.

We were also able to have a public excavation day that was open to members of the community on a weekend, near the end of the field season when student volunteers were sufficiently competent to instruct and supervise the participants doing the excavating. We restricted excavations to the peripheral areas of the midden, after we assured ourselves that we had almost certainly excavated the key portions.

Dozens of public presentations and exhibits have featured artifacts from the Suicide Creek site; local print media gave some attention, and a television news program did a feature focusing on the K–12 programming at the site. The site was also the primary focus of a 45-minute documentary on logging in the area during the early twentieth century, which ran on a cable television station at least dozens of times.

STORIES FROM THE FIELD

Rain and bears were constant while we were at Suicide Creek. We never had a shelter at the site, so there was no escaping the rain. We just worked through it. We never had any proper benches or chairs to sit on either; usually we just sat on the ground or on logs. Students were often warned that sitting on a moss-covered log, while tempting, was also risky, as broken glass or nails could be hidden under the moss. Nevertheless, some people needed to learn the hard way. No injuries resulted, though. On occasion, someone would run the metal detector over any log we wanted to sit on, as a precaution.

We saw lots of bears while we worked near Suicide Creek, but they never came on site. They were noticed close to the trailhead of the site, but there were never any serious encounters. On occasion, visiting adults were visibly nervous. One such visitor has gone on to a successful career in archaeology, and I often wonder how he managed to control his fear of bears.

While working at and near Suicide Creek, we consulted foresters frequently. One time, Eric Crossin (the retired forester who showed us the site), a field school student, and I were doing some survey work in the area, beyond the site itself, mostly on a mountainside. Later, the student told me how funny it was working with us: "Eric was always looking up, you were always looking down, and I was looking straight ahead to see where we were going." Eric would have been consciously or unconsciously looking up, after a career in the forests spent identifying trees; I was consciously looking for evidence of artifacts or features. The student was making sure we weren't getting lost.

It was interesting having a group of four professional foresters at the site for one day. Walking up the access trail with them, I said, "About 40 meters after the big maple tree, we will be turning right and bushwhacking to the site." For the rest of the walk in, the foresters debated the value of the maple. According to them, it was likely worth close to $100,000, and they were wondering why nobody had come in and cut it down. Foresters apparently think differently than archaeologists, who would rarely consider the monetary value of such things. Once we got on site and I was showing them around, I mentioned that I hoped to be able to get a corer (a metal hollow tube to drill into a tree), so I could determine the age of the trees growing on top of the features. They told me to just cut the tree down and count the rings. "Of course, it would be illegal but nobody would see or hear you up here." I think they were joking, but I'm not sure.

The foresters taught me a lot of valuable things, especially how quickly trees grow in the valley. I also gained some insight into how quickly some species decompose. The forest is dominated by cedar, fir, and hemlock trees. Mostly cedar and fir trees were logged. Cedar is common for building because it splits nicely and preserves well. There was considerably evidence of cedar planking at the Suicide Creek site, some with nails sticking out of the planks. I asked the foresters whether it was reasonable to think that if some of the building materials had been made of fir or hemlock, they would now be decomposed while the cedar remained. They all agreed that it was indeed reasonable.

5

A Most Unusual Site near McKenzie Creek

Visitor to site, after learning it was a Nikkei logging camp:
　　Where's the ofuro?
Dumbfounded archaeologist: Excuse me?
Visitor: Where's the ofuro?
Archaeologist: What's an ofuro?
Visitor: Japanese bathhouse.
　　　– Conversation between a visitor to the McKenzie Creek
　　　　site and a sheepish and embarrassed project director

INTRODUCTION

It is common practice for archaeological sites to have an official site designation, consisting of a series of numbers and/or letters issued by a governing authority, such as a province or state. It is also common, however, that sites are given names by archaeologists, often based on location. Such was the case with the Suicide Creek site described in the last chapter. And that was the case with the McKenzie Creek site as well. (This naming is unlike that used for the settler sites described in

Chapter 3, which were named for known occupiers, such as the Fowlers, Martin/McKay, or Hastings/Sparks sites, or based on locally used place names, such as "The Point" site.)

One of the problems in archaeology is identifying the precise location of a site since doing so could lead to looting by pothunters. The McKenzie Creek site is relatively close to McKenzie Creek, but it is not the most obvious choice of a geographic location for a site name. It was given the name to provide a general location but hopefully not one specific enough to make it easy for pothunters to find.

Unofficial site names are sometimes subject to change. As described elsewhere (Chapter 4), this site was almost certainly occupied by Nikkei, and the logging operation on site was probably established and run by a prominent Nikkei person in early twentieth century British Columbia – Eikichi Kagetsu. Consequently, while this site is most often referred to as the McKenzie Creek site, it is sometimes known as the Nikkei Camp or the Kagetsu Camp in the Seymour Valley, depending on context. On the British Columbia Register of Historic Places, the site is called the "Seymour Valley Camp." The provincial government has designated it DiRi 25.

During discussions with Tadashi (Jack) Kagetsu, mentioned in Chapter 4, he indicated his father had established a Nikkei logging camp somewhere close to Lot 922. Lot 922 is only a few hundred meters from the location of the McKenzie Creek site.

The project shifted focus from the Suicide Creek site to the McKenzie Creek site because access to the Suicide Creek location was going to be restricted, at least for a field season or two.

During our time in the LSCR, there were multiple large and ongoing construction projects, such as the building of a filtration plant, the excavation of tunnels for water pipes, and the maintenance of the dam. This meant that access to some of our sites was, on occasion, temporarily restricted. Knowing that we were focusing on a logging camp at Suicide Creek, a supervisor in the LSCR suggested another site we might be interested in investigating, a probable logging camp recently identified close to a newly constructed pathway. Eventually, we would work elsewhere, back at the Suicide Creek site on occasion and at the settler sites doing regular bits of work, but work at this newly discovered site would be the primary focus of the project moving forward. The site appeared to have been a logging camp established by and for Nikkei for a few years around 1920; apparently, the camp transitioned to a more permanent settlement in the forest and remained there for another couple of decades, until the forced removal of Nikkei from the coastal region and their placement in internment camps beginning in 1942.

The McKenzie Creek site is very significant and has received more attention than any of the other sites investigated by the project. This chapter provides an overview of the project's initial investigations and of the site's features. It also tells a few related stories from the field and documents some early confusion about the site. Chapter 6, in turn, provides more details about the site's excavation, artifacts, and significance and presents its usefulness to public archaeology, as well as a few more stories from the field. In part, Chapter 7 draws inferences from the investigations at the McKenzie Creek site. This amount of detail is warranted because of the site's significance and the fact that fieldwork occurred at McKenzie Creek over nine field seasons.

Keeping with the theme of the culture of fieldwork, this chapter also includes a box on fieldwork, food, and music (see Box 5.1 near the end of this chapter).

DISCOVERY AND INITIAL ASSESSMENT

When the LSCR supervisor showed me the site, it immediately struck me as an excellent fit for the Seymour Valley Archaeology Project. It had direct and easy access along a paved pathway (which would make it easy for students to get to, as well as the public). One of the reasons I wanted to go to Suicide Creek to excavate was to gain some experience in historical archaeology without being under the watchful eye of the public. After a few seasons excavating at the Suicide Creek site, I was confident enough about excavating historic period sites, including logging camps, not to worry about being in public view. I also wanted to continue the focus on logging camps, and this site would serve that purpose well. As with the Suicide Creek site, the McKenzie Creek site gave no initial indications that it was a Nikkei logging camp. We knew that Eikichi Kagetsu had logging operations somewhere close by, but there were no surface indications that this was his camp.

When the supervisor was showing the site, he said that it was discovered when the paved pathway was being constructed, and they altered the course of the pathway to avoid the site. A few months later, while at the location with another supervisor (but months before excavations began), I discovered that the last time LSCR staff members had been at the site, they had seen many bottles scattered about. These were gone. The site was apparently being looted by people using the path, which, it turns out, did not avoid the site. It bisected it. So although the site initially had high archaeological visibility because of all the bottles on view, by the time I saw the site for the first time, it had no archaeological visibility from the pathway. Presumably all these bottles had been looted.

I would come to learn only after we began our work at the site that there had been an archaeological impact assessment done prior to the start of the Seymour Valley Archaeology Project. I had obtained copies of a few other impact assessments conducted in the LSCR, but the one identifying this site was initially missed. I learned of it by chance one day when speaking with one of the archaeologists who worked on the project.

In advance of constructing a 10 km (6.2 mile) paved pathway running roughly north-south through the LSCR, Metro Vancouver contracted an archaeology consulting company to do an archaeological impact assessment, and the archaeologist forwarded me a copy. The report reads, in part, "Corridor crosses an old logging camp. Several pit features, rock retaining walls, historic debris including glass fragments, metal pot fragments, old shoes, saws. Also saw remains of saki bottles inscribed with Japanese characters. Pathway will avoid historic features and debris" (Arcas Consulting 1999, 19).

Because archaeological impact assessments focused on pre-1846 sites in British Columbia at that time, there were no more specific details provided about the site. Even the geographic location was vague.

Once the pathway was constructed, the site was apparently easy pickings for pothunters.

While we were still excavating at the Suicide Creek site, we moved over to the newly discovered McKenzie Creek site to do some more focused assessment. We had been led to believe the camp was to the east of the new paved pathway, so we focused attention there. Students undertook an intensive surface survey through the area, following transects that ran west to east. Some parts of the area were densely vegetated, and the terrain in places was difficult to traverse. Such was the difficulty that it took 15 students a full day to do the survey, with transects usually less than 150 meters in length.

The results of the survey were interesting. One student discovered an almost complete Japanese rice bowl, triggering thoughts of "Here we go again. Another unexpected Nikkei camp." Other students discovered scattered pieces of metal and broken glass and identified some cultural depressions and part of a rock wall. At the time, we were not aware of the archaeological impact assessment that had been done previously, but we saw the same things, except most of the surface artifacts had been looted.

Although told that the camp was on the east side of the pathway, we realized that the archaeologists who did the initial impact assessment probably spent little time on site and that the workers in the LSCR were not trained in identifying archaeological sites. So we decided to also have a look on the west side of the pathway. Sure enough, we spotted a hole, on a naturally elevated space a few meters west of the pathway. The hole was rectangular, measuring about 3 meters by 2 meters (9 by 6 feet). The hole appeared to have been recently filled with branches and brush, presumably debris from the construction of the pathway. I explained to the students that rectangular holes rarely occur in nature so this was worth investigating.

A couple of students volunteered to clear the square hole of debris. It was tough. In addition to the branches and debris, they had to remove a live wasp nest and many rocks. It was obvious that this was an artificially created hole; each wall went straight down. At a depth of about 1.5 meters below the ground surface, the students had finished clearing the debris and were able to continue excavating with shovels. At the end of the second day, they struck a wooden pole placed vertically in one of the corners, then another. A few more minutes of excavating revealed nails in one of the poles. Finally, we had hard evidence that this was a cultural creation. Often in archaeology, some of the most interesting and potentially significant discoveries happen during the last days or hours of a field project. And so it was in this case. Time had run out. A few minutes after discovering the post with nails, we had to close down our investigations at the McKenzie Creek site for the season. Eventually, we were able to continue excavations in subsequent years and determine that this was a water reservoir lined with cedar planks. The reservoir is described more completely in the section of this chapter entitled "The Features at McKenzie Creek."

During our initial investigations, we also did some surface surveying in the areas to the north, to the south, and to the west of the site. We didn't bother with surveying to the east because there was a distinct bluff in that direction. To the north, we discovered evidence of a cedar plank road leading directly to Lot 922, which supported the notion that this was a Kagetsu camp. To the south, we discovered a road or pathway that ran a few hundred meters, which likely connected to other roads in the early twentieth century. To the west was a steep mountainside, which had much evidence of skid roads, built for skidding large timbers out of the forest. Some of these skid roads led directly to the site.

Ultimately, after our two days of initial fieldwork, we were satisfied that this was an early twentieth century logging camp. The discovery of a single rice bowl suggested there may have been some Nikkei workers in the camp, but we had no idea of what was to come – that McKenzie Creek was a highly significant site that began as a short-term Nikkei logging camp but likely transitioned to a more permanent settlement for Nikkei, a settlement undocumented and unknown to most, and eventually forgotten.

Our initial investigations also indicated that the new paved pathway bisected the site. About 90 per cent of the site is to the east of the pathway. Construction of the pathway destroyed about 400 square meters of the site.

Documentary research indicated that the site was on property owned by the Hastings Company in the early years of the twentieth century. We think that company logged the area, using skid roads, in the first decade of the century. We further think that when Kagetsu received permission to log Lot 922, he visited the area and determined it was a good location for a camp: it was already tied into a road network, it was flat (unlike most of the area), and it had a plentiful supply of water from the freshwater creeks nearby. We also surveyed Lot 922, but found no evidence of a camp.

THE FEATURES AT MCKENZIE CREEK

Figure 5.1 is a map of the site, showing the locations of features. Figure 5.2 is a sketch of how the site might have looked when it was occupied.

Two Roads. We identified two roads within the boundaries of the site. One is a skid road. Some logs are now missing, but originally the skid road would have been comprised of a series of short sections of logs (about 2 meters or 6 feet in length) placed several meters apart, parallel to one another but perpendicular to the direction of travel. These roads

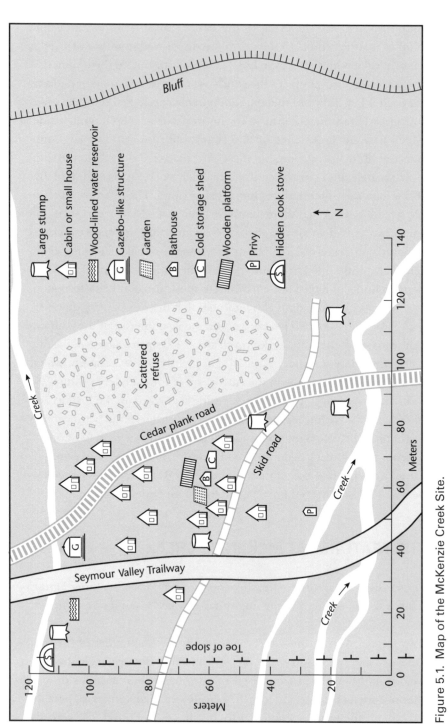

Figure 5.1. Map of the McKenzie Creek Site.

Figure 5.2. Reconstruction Drawing of the McKenzie Creek Logging Camp, circa 1920. Credit: K. Cook.

were used to skid large timbers out of the forest. The logs being skidded would have been pulled by a horse. The skid road at the site connected with the skid roads on the mountainside to the west of the site.

The other road was a cedar plank road. This was likely constructed by workers for Eikichi Kagetsu, whose logging practices in this area focused on shingle bolt logging. (Shingle bolts are the sections of logs from which wooden shingles are made.) Rather than skidding tall timbers over skid roads, the loggers working for him used sleds to haul shingle bolts over cedar plank roads. The cedar plank road doubled as a boardwalk for pedestrian traffic through the site.

The Ofuro (Bathhouse). The ofuro had very low archaeological visibility but was discovered after a Nikkei visitor to the site asked where it was – she was so certain that there would be one. The story of the discovery is detailed later in this chapter, and its excavation is described in Chapter 6. In short, we discovered the foundation of the ofuro, which had a rectangular shape with three sides of rock and one side open. Inside this space, a fire would have burned. A tub with a metal base and wood walls would have been placed over the fire, resting on the three rock walls. A building would have been constructed around the structure. The base of the tub would have measured about 1.2 meters by 1.2 meters (4 by 4 feet), and the tub itself was probably about 1.2 meters (4 feet) high. The open end of the rock structure was so that the fire could have been fed from outside the building.

We discovered the entire base of the ofuro, all three walls. We also observed charred wood from the fire. Close by, we found sections of pipes that brought water to the tub, and we also found a small portion of the tub itself. Other artifacts recovered from excavations around the ofuro are discussed in Chapter 6.

The Water Reservoir. This feature, originally discovered in the first days of investigation, was a deep rectangular hole, measuring 2 meters (6'6") in width, 3 meters (9'10") in length, and 2.5 meters (8'2") in depth. There were vertical posts in each corner and vertical cedar planking covering each wall, held in place with wood cross rails. The reservoir was fed by an underground stream, so the reservoir filled with water as we removed sediments. This feature was at the high point of the site, and very few other artifacts or features were nearby. Considering the discovery of pipes found elsewhere on the site, pipes presumably used for carrying water, we believe this feature was a water reservoir that fed water to the rest of the camp through pipes via gravity.

The Privy. Near the southern boundary of the site was a rectangular depression, measuring 3 meters (9'10") in length by 0.85 meters (2'9") in width. The depression before excavation was 0.9 meters (2'9") deep. We didn't excavate it right away; we left it for a few seasons. Whenever I showed it to students or visitors, I would tell them what we knew: "It's almost certainly cultural, because rectangular holes are very rare in nature; it might be a privy, but we won't know until we excavate."

Eventually, we did excavate it, to a depth of 1.5 meters. The method of its excavation and the recovered artifacts, mostly bottles, we found are described in Chapter 6. Based on the location of the feature (on the periphery of the site), the size and shape of the feature, and the contents (i.e., empty bottles), we infer that this was a **privy**.

Figure 5.3. Excavating in the Garden Area of the McKenzie Creek Site. Credit: R. Muckle.

The Garden. A relatively flat area of the site, about 4 meters square, was located immediately west of the ofuro. We initially assumed, because of its size and flatness, that it was the location of a cabin or small house. It turned out, however, that it was almost certainly a garden. We found few artifacts here, and the sediments included dense quantities of small fragments of animal bone, which we assume were used to enhance the soil for growing.

A Gazebo-Like Structure. There is a rock feature close to the northern boundary of the site. We describe it as a gazebo-like structure, but we aren't really sure what its function was. It is comprised of four rock walls forming a square. Each wall is about 2 meters in length and about 60 cm (2 feet) in height. There has been some alteration to the original structure, caused by some slumping into the creek. The western wall was also buried by the construction of the paved pathway. At one time, cedar planks were laid over the rock walls, creating a wooden platform with a rock wall base. Artifacts found within and around this feature were scarce. Within the feature, we found part of a lantern and some twisted wire, which we

BOX 5.1 FIELDWORK, FOOD, AND MUSIC

Over the course of the Seymour Valley Archaeology Project, we held more than 300 communal lunches while doing fieldwork. The primary topic of conversation at almost every one of these lunches was food. It also became apparent that many of the students had strong backgrounds in music; indeed, many were or became professional musicians. The link between archaeology and music was clear to several.

Food

Food is a big thing in fieldwork. Nobody could complain about the food on the Seymour Valley Archaeology Project because each student was responsible for his or her own.

The food habits of students roughly paralleled global concerns about food and packaging. There were seasons, mostly in the early years, when meat sandwiches were the norm. In the later years, lunches including meat were less common. In the early years, most students had sandwiches wrapped in cellophane and brought prepackaged commercial snacks, like cookies or candy bars. Beverages were almost always in disposable containers too. In later years, almost all the students brought their food in reusable plastic or glass containers, and snacks were mostly fruit and vegetables. Beverages were also in reusable containers. Salads became a big thing in later years.

When some students forgot to bring cutlery and had a meal requiring it, they used their trowels. The project director neither approved of nor recommended this practice.

Working toward a sustainable archaeology, we conducted waste audits for the project in 2013 and 2019. Major categories were "project waste," which mostly included packaging from supplies and the supplies themselves, such as used flagging tape, and "personal waste," which was mostly food waste from lunches and snacks. In both 2013 and 2019, the food waste was negligible. There was very little waste of food, and only a bit of discarded food packaging. It is likely that the total food waste could have fit in a one-gallon bucket.

One field school student was a professional chef. Sadly, he never offered to cook a meal for us. Another student had a relative who owned a sandwich shop, which graciously supplied dozens of foot-long sandwiches, and another student worked at a coffee shop, so we had a steady supply of free freshly brewed coffee every day for that field season.

There were often special "food treat" days, which students organized themselves. It was a regular occurrence, for example, to have a donut day, and on somebody's birthday, it was common to have cake.

Music

It came to light that many of the field school students were, or had been, heavily involved in the music industry. Not being a musician, I often wondered about the connection, so I asked some former field school students about it.

Dr. Chris Springer, now a consulting archaeologist, came from a career as a musician (in the genre of fusion) and is well known in the local music industry. He was quick to point out the similarities in lifestyle, likening archaeologists in the field to musicians touring or performing a gig. It was the lifestyle, being and working together – each playing a particular part – over days and weeks. Intense and fun!

Former field school student Jon Sheppard has similarly made a career in consulting archaeology while also working with his band, the Living Room Project, which creates and performs music he describes as "alternative bluesy electronic rock." He too sees the similarities between fieldwork and touring: "Both entail long sleepless nights in questionable motel rooms shared with several other people, on a diet of mainly coffee and beer, in small towns that most people have not even heard of...." Jon further sees a connection between archaeological fieldwork and making music:

> It's about making something from nothing. When you show up at a site, there is often no indication of what's below.... Gradually, you scrape with your trowel or shovel, and the site reveals itself to you ... it [is] similar with music, wherein you begin with literally nothing, and note by note the song essentially reveals itself to you.

The similarity of fieldwork and songwriting was also foremost in the minds of field school students Carmen Bruno and Jane Sawyer. Bruno is a singer/songwriter with TrailerHawk, a band that performs Southern rock, a subgenre of Americana. She continued to get a degree and work in archaeology after the field school. Here is her comparison of archaeological excavation and songwriting: "In both cases you are trying to understand what we do, why we do it, and how we feel about it. Writing a song is much like digging for answers."

Sawyer, who was formerly a singer/songwriter for the indie rock band Dick'n'Jane, also compares musical creation with archaeological fieldwork:

> As a songwriter, I sought to imbue the ordinary with meaning ... and connect to the audience. In a similar way, archaeologists mine the mundane, everyday objects of human life, so we can reach back, empathize, and connect.... There is also the business of creating music with other people that shares the same arena as archaeology. Collaboration is as old as dirt. As well, bands are always working the mode of discovery, always on the edge of coming up with something new while, at the same time, keenly aware that music itself ... is as old as time. Musicians, like archaeologists, do not so much create new things but rather they give new meaning to old things.

assume was used to hang the lantern. We assume, but do not really know, that there may have been posts and a roof. Lack of nails or window glass around the feature persuades us there was no substantial structure here, such as one with walls. Some suggest this may have been a shrine. Others suggest it may have been a washing area. We really don't know.

Cold Storage Building. Immediately east of the ofuro, we found evidence of a building with a pit inside. The discovery of nails and window glass indicate the building was about 2.5 by 2.5 meters (about 8 by 8 feet). Within the building was a square pit, measuring 1.5 by 1.5 meters on the surface and reaching a depth of 1 meter. We found no artifacts within the dimensions of the building or the hole that might lead us to interpreting this feature's function. We surmise that it may have been used for cold storage. An alternative explanation is that it is a privy, but its location in a central part of the site, adjacent to the ofuro, lessens that likelihood, as does the presence of a privy close to the southern boundary of the site.

Cabins or Small Houses. More than a dozen areas have been identified as the locations of cabins or small houses. The inference that they were cabins or small houses is based primarily on the evidence we found in or near them: nails and window glass; clusters of household artifacts, such as dishes, bottles, and stove pieces; and personal items, such as clothing (as evidenced by buttons), timepieces, and toothbrushes.

CONFUSION RUNS RAMPANT

The first several weeks of fieldwork at the site, spread over two years, was a confusing time. A lot of what we were seeing didn't make sense. We were able to see that it was logging camp, but it was like no logging camp I was familiar with – either in the historical research or based on the work at the Suicide Creek site. Where was the bunkhouse? Where was the kitchen and central eating area? Where was the trash midden? We couldn't find any evidence that suggested any of these things. Instead, everything seemed scattered. I often wondered whether the site had been badly disturbed. Perhaps that disturbance had scattered the evidence of the bunkhouse, the cooking and eating areas, and the midden. I asked many visitors to the site what they thought. Did the site look disturbed? I asked several archaeologists and a few geographers. The consensus was that the site did not look disturbed, either by nature or people.

Then I had an "ah ha" moment when everything made sense. One evening during the second field season at the site, I was reading about a camp associated with a logging mill in Washington State. The reports indicated that most of the workers lived in bunkhouses, but there was also a contingent of Japanese workers who lived on the periphery of the camp, in houses with their families. Reading that put everything in perspective. There was no bunkhouse, there was no central cooking and eating area, there was no central trash midden. In this camp, each Japanese logger lived in a cabin or small house with his family.

It was a turning point. During and between the initial field seasons, students and I continued researching Nikkei logging practices, trying to support the view that this was indeed such a camp. We found multiple references, usually based on memoirs, of Nikkei living in camps during the early twentieth century, but these sources generally supported the notion that mostly men lived in a bunkhouse with a few women who served as cooks, servers, and cleaners. We did a deeper dive into the historical research, though, and found some research supporting the idea that loggers may have lived with their families at McKenzie Creek. A master's thesis written in 1935 indicated that, according to a survey of those Nikkei in British Columbia working in the industry in 1924, 34 per cent lived with their families in the camps (Sumida 1935). We also discovered a local history book (for a community in a different region of the province) that mentioned a Nikkei logging camp (Olson 2004). The book includes memories of the camp, which indicate that, although there was a bunkhouse and cookhouse for the males without families, there were also small houses or cabins for those who chose to live with their families. Further, these memories place a communal bathhouse, a water system, and gardens in that camp. Remarkably, this camp was also operated by Eikichi Kagetsu. After he closed his operations in the Seymour Valley in the early 1920s, he moved to Vancouver Island and established what was, apparently, a similarly structured camp as that at McKenzie Creek. We became very confident in our interpretations that this was a camp in which loggers lived with their families.

STORIES FROM THE FIELD

The epigraph of this chapter – "*Where's the ofuro?*" – is key to the research at the site.

One evening during the first full field season at the site, I gave a presentation on the site to a community group. A few days later, I received a request from a woman (Kathy Stubbs) who was in attendance, asking if she and some others from another group she was active in could come for a site tour. A few days later, a group of several women showed up for the tour. I gave them the full tour, which lasted about 45 minutes, and I concluded with the statement that this was very likely a Nikkei logging camp occupied for a few years around 1920. One of the women in the group, Irene Nemeth, asked, "Where's the ofuro?" I was embarrassed. I didn't even know what an ofuro was. Irene, who was Nikkei herself and certain there would be an ofuro on site, described what one would look like. This led to a very sleepless night. I had many doubts about my competence as an archaeologist – here I am directing excavations at a Nikkei site, the second one I've excavated no less, and I don't even know what an ofuro is. In fairness, though, I never set out to work on a Nikkei site. I was never looking for Nikkei sites. The following morning, I was driven to somehow make up for my incompetence. I was determined to discover the ofuro, and I did. The base of the ofuro, the rock structure upon which the tub would sit, was like the tip of an iceberg. The entire site is quite rocky, but I noticed a pattern in a few of the rocks poking through the surface. Later that day, I got in touch with many historical archaeologists through an online listserv and eventually found myself communicating with some of the major players in Asian American archaeology. I was looking for advice on excavating an ofuro. At the time, nobody was aware of any that had been excavated and wished us luck. Details of the excavation and what we found are described in Chapter 6.

There is a similar story regarding the garden. Archaeologist Suzanne Villeneuve was on one of her multiple visits to the site one day, this time bringing her mom – Sharon Villeneuve. When we were at the flattened area west of the ofuro, I said it was probably the location of a house. Sharon, who had an interest in Nikkei culture, suggested it might have been a garden. Over the next few years, I continued to think it was probably the location of a building, but I never totally dismissed the idea that it might be a garden. During one field season, students created an unintentional path through the flattened area by carrying buckets of excavated sediments to be sifted. It didn't take long before we could see dense concentrations of small fragments of animal bones. We immediately stopped walking through the area, but I still didn't know what to make of the bones. A short time later, Doug Ross (an expert in Asian American archaeology) was visiting the site and suggested the bone pieces may have been placed in the ground to enrich the soil, a known practice at other Nikkei sites in North America. Sharon Villeneuve was right. It was a garden.

6

Digging In at McKenzie Creek

By its very nature, archaeological excavation is destructive, and careful attention should be given to both the location and extent of the digging.

– Muckle and Camp (2021, 111)

INTRODUCTION

It took a while to figure out this was a unique site. Things were made easier once we realized that the McKenzie Creek site had been a logging camp with multiple cabins or small houses rather than a more typical camp like others established in the region during the early twentieth century, including at Suicide Creek, which had one or more bunkhouses and communal eating areas. Once we identified many of the obvious features, even though we weren't necessarily certain of their function, we turned attention more fully to excavation.

In total, the Seymour Valley Archaeology Project spent parts or all of nine field seasons at the McKenzie Creek site, mostly excavating. Overall, the site is about the size of a football field. We excavated about 15 per cent of it.

This chapter focuses on excavation at the site – the strategies, methods, and results. Excavations suggested that after its initial use as a logging camp, the site transitioned to a more permanent settlement in the forest, which was largely unknown and eventually forgotten. Some of the artifacts and their contexts supporting this inference are introduced in this chapter and discussed more fully in Chapter 7. This chapter also includes a discussion of the significance of the site and of the public archaeology associated with it.

EXCAVATION STRATEGIES AND METHODS

The principal objective of the excavations at the McKenzie Creek site was to determine the layout of the site, including the number of structures, the kinds of structures, and how they were related. During the fieldwork over several seasons, our strategies changed as our understanding of the site changed. We began looking for different kinds of structures and artifacts, for example, after we understood that what had been a logging camp likely transitioned to a more permanent settlement in the forest. Excavations largely remained focused on features though – including on those that were obvious, such as those described in Chapter 5. But we also excavated to find more features. While the initial investigation focused on the layout of the site, subsequent excavations were focused on finding evidence associated with gender, children, maintaining ethnic identity, and, most important, finding evidence to support the hypothesis of an ongoing occupation at the site for about 20 years after its use as a logging camp, an occupation that ended only with the forced removal of Nikkei from the region in 1942.

The places of excavation were mostly chosen judgmentally, based primarily on evidence of cultural material on the ground surface and in test pits. Those areas deemed most likely, in the opinion of the project director, to have subsurface evidence of human activities were selected. Because we wanted to determine or confirm the function of the obvious features, we chose to excavate those first. Because we wanted to find the locations of other features with low or no archaeological visibility, we often chose where to excavate based on surface artifacts. We recognized the limitations of judgmental sampling, though, especially in a forest with mostly uneven terrain, so we also did some probabilistic sampling. We put in small test pits, about 30 cm (12 inch) square, at 20-meter intervals through much of the site. Many of these test pits produced cultural remains, and we chose a few to orient further excavations. We began excavating near these test pits in units that were 2 meters by 2 meters and then expanded when we found evidence that we were probably excavating a cabin or small house.

Excavations were mostly done to 5 or 10 cm arbitrary levels, by trowel, and sediments were sifted through 6 mm (1/4 inch) mesh screens. The obvious features were mostly excavated using the boundaries of the features themselves, or the presumed boundaries, such as a potential building structure surrounding a feature. Excavations done elsewhere on site were done in 2-meter by 2-meter units as well. Artifacts were recorded in situ. Items that did not meet the criteria of being classified as an artifact for this site, such as nails and undiagnostic pieces of metal, glass, and ceramics, were collected in **level bags**. All students kept detailed records of their excavation work in field notebooks (see Box 6.1).

EXCAVATING THE OBVIOUS FEATURES

The Water Reservoir. As described in Chapter 5, the first feature we started to excavate at the site, during the initial investigation of the site, was the water reservoir. Most of this excavation was done by shovel, except along the walls where trowels were used so as not to damage the wooden walls. Students needed a ladder to get into and out of the unit. Once we got to about 2 meters below surface, we put shoring in to prevent the walls from collapsing on excavators. We also created a pulley system to lift the heavy buckets of sediment out of the unit. We found no artifacts within the water reservoir. Excavations went to the bottom of the reservoir's wooden walls, which lay on top of hard, compacted clay. Excavations were particularly difficult near the bottom of the unit, as it continually filled with water and we needed to bail water frequently while excavating.

Excavating the Ofuro. Excavating the ofuro was interesting and more than a bit nerve-racking, at least in the beginning. As mentioned in Chapter 5, after I had consulted with other archaeologists working on Asian American sites, it was evident that this might be the first ofuro excavated in North America. After we had exposed the top of the

BOX 6.1 NOTES FROM THE FIELD

Field notes are routinely kept by an archaeology project director, as well as by all members of the crew. At a minimum, they are a daily record of each individual's work and thoughts in the day. Often, entries are made throughout the day, while one is surveying or excavating. Sometimes, they provide a broad overview of work and thoughts, but at other times, they focus on specific details, such as the precise location of an artifact. Maps and sketches are common in field notes.

Field notes are some of the raw data of an archaeological field project. They are often archived with the other project records.

All students in the Seymour Valley Archaeology Project kept field notes. Considering the weather, they wrote field notes in waterproof field notebooks. Students typically made three or four entries throughout each day in the field, and then spent the last 15 minutes of the day summarizing the day's work.

How to write proper field notes was incorporated into what the field school students learned. One of the most important things taught was that the field notes had to be legible. Students had to write so that their notes could be read easily by others, 100 years or more in the future.

This is an example of an excerpt summarizing the work one student did one day. It's good in the sense that it provides a combination of details about the excavation and finds and lets the reader know what the student is thinking:

> ... excavating by 5 cm levels. We found lots of charred wood, 4 nails, a circular-shaped piece of metal (detailed in catalog) and melted glass. Our hypothesis is that this was a cabin.

Most of the field notes for any day should focus on the archaeology, but students were not discouraged from including some non-archaeology things as well. For example, field books often included comments about animals seen that day, and food: "... found a salamander.... Today is ... birthday so we had cake at lunchtime."

This is a good example of an entry made following the completion of a single excavation level:

> The coordinates of the unit are 20–18S; 6.3–8.3E. We excavated the 35–40 cm level. I found 33 pieces of aqua colored glass near the southern edge of the unit. I saw of piece of bottleneck near the edge of a rock and pushed the rock a little aside. I found almost half a bottle. I have sketched the unit. I put the pieces in a level bag.

Writing about the weather was not discouraged either: "Today was a very rainy day.... everyone was soaking wet."

Figure 6.1 shows field school students making detailed records and writing field notes following their discovery of an artifact while excavating at the McKenzie Creek site.

foundation holding the tub, Irene Nemeth, who had first mentioned that there would be an ofuro, agreed to come back to the site to take a look. She confirmed that it was an ofuro.

We exposed the entire foundation of the ofuro and found charred wood from the fire used to heat the water in the tub, as well as a piece of the tub itself – a piece of the metal floor nailed into part of the wooden side. There were few artifacts found associated with the ofuro, but the ones we did find were interesting. We found a metal ladle, which people likely used to transfer some water from the tub to a basin from which they would wash themselves before getting in the tub. We also found a metal basin and several small pieces of a hard plastic-like material (maybe Bakelite). The last piece of this material we found had writing: "Eastman Kodak – Bulls Eye." The pieces came from a camera. We found several hundred nails of various sizes around the perimeter of the feature, almost certainly from the walls and roof. We found metal pipes leading to the ofuro, presumably linked to the water reservoir and used to fill the tub when necessary.

Figure 6.1. Recording Artifacts and Writing Field Notes. Credit: R. Muckle.

Pictured in Figure 6.2 is a student documenting the exposure of the base of the ofuro (Japanese bathhouse), a horseshoe-shaped rock feature that would have supported a tub of water heated by a wood fire below. The entire structure would have been enclosed in a wood building.

The Privy. The privy excavation was tough, mostly occurring over two days of very heavy rain. Like the water reservoir excavation, it was difficult digging. After removing the recent debris, comprised mostly of branches and other vegetation, students took to using shovels mainly. Several times during the first day of excavation, the students excavating declared that the spot was sterile, to which I always replied that the project director declares when a unit is sterile, not them. I also continually reminded them of why we were digging, saying, "Rectangular holes like this rarely occur in nature, so keep digging." I didn't blame them; it was difficult digging with lots of rocks to be moved.

Near the end of the first day, just after I had finished a "keep digging" pep talk and was leaving the excavation, I had walked no more than 4 or 5 meters away when I heard a "clink" – the sound of a metal shovel on glass. Over the rest of that day and all of the next, we recovered dozens of

Figure 6.2. Excavating the Ofuro. Credit: Nicki Simon.

artifacts, including 29 complete bottles, 4 broken ones, a canning jar, and dozens of fragments of metal cans. The bottles were mostly tightly packed in the central part of the pit. We assume they were dropped down the hole and, with the presumably soft landing provided in a privy, did not break.

The Gazebo-Like Structure. One season, we put a small test pit, about 50 cm (20 inches) square, in the center of the gazebo-like structure. It was sterile. In a subsequent field season, we excavated with trowels the entire inside area of the four rock walls defining the feature. After removing the top few centimeters of sediment, we saw decomposing cedar planks. We could see that despite the barely perceptible condition the planks were now in, they created a solid wood platform over the rock wall base. Excavations revealed few artifacts. In one corner, a few centimeters below the surface, we discovered an approximately 15 cm (6 inch) length of twisted wire and a few pieces of curved glass that we presume were from a lantern. We found several nails in the unit as well, which we presume were from a collapsed roof. Excavating around the perimeter revealed no other artifacts. If there had been a building with walls, we expect that we would have seen nails, but there were none. Consequently, we imagined this to be a gazebo-like structure with a rock wall base and perhaps a roof; the lantern, we thought, must have hung from one corner of the roof.

The Garden. As mentioned in the previous chapter, we initially thought that the flattened area near the ofuro was probably the location of a cabin or small house. After we discovered high densities of fragmented bone, however, we accepted that it was probably a garden. We excavated part of the area in anticipation of finding botanical remains to see what they were growing. We never found botanical remains, but we did find an accumulation of a few dozen nails. We think these nails could be the remains of a bench or other small structure that one might find in a garden. While excavating, a student called me over to ask a very common question posed by field school students. Holding up what appeared to be a pebble encased in dirt, she asked, "Is this anything?" I said, "Probably just a pebble." But after handling it, I said, "It seems a bit light for a pebble, though, so I will go clean it up with water and let you know." When it got wet, my hand turned black. It was a nodule of graphite. Further, the graphite was beveled, indicating it had been used, probably for sketching. Two of the students that year were familiar with Japanese art and culture, and they both got excited. We had discovered what they called a "sumi stick," used for drawing.

EXCAVATING ELSEWHERE

Hoping to find residences (cabins or small houses), we often chose to excavate where there were surface indications that such a residence had existed. These clues included, for example, the leg of a cookstove or a piece of window glass poking through the ground. Sometimes we were successful in finding a residence and sometimes not. Sometimes it was just scattered trash. Opening up a 2 by 2 meter excavation unit often did lead to finding a residence, though; we believe we found 14 distinct residences on site. We determined they were residences based primarily on our retrieval of distinct clusters of household and personal items, such as dishes, stoves, remnants of clothing (e.g., buttons and footwear), lanterns, toothbrushes, and timepieces.

There was one cluster of household artifacts with no dishes, except for one of the very few Western-style cups we discovered on site. While a Nikkei woman was visiting the site one day, I mentioned that I was looking for evidence of women at the site and showed her many of the cosmetic containers we had discovered, suggesting this was one line of evidence. She said that the cosmetic containers were not, in fact, good indications of women at the site because even if hand lotions or creams were marketed to women, the men wouldn't care. They would use whatever worked. She added, "Besides, you have lots of other evidence of women here." Gesturing toward the many Japanese dishes on display at the site, she said, "It's the dishes. These are really nice dishes, indicating women were here. If it were just Japanese men, they would be eating out of cans and using a Western-style cup." From that point on, we referred to the cluster of household items without dishes as the "Bachelor Cabin."

THE ARTIFACTS

Close to 1,000 artifacts were recovered from the McKenzie Creek site. These include evidence of almost 200 different bottles, more than 100 cans, several dozen Japanese dishes, and at least 31 cosmetic jars, as well as industrial artifacts, portions of metal stoves, lanterns, and many personal items. Several coins were excavated, all dating between 1900 and 1918.

The bottles are of various kinds. There are beer bottles, some for local beers and some for beers imported from Japan. There are dozens of medicine or pharmaceutical bottles; as with the beer bottles, some were local and others were inscribed with Japanese characters. There were also bottles with Japanese inscriptions indicating they once held sake. Four ink bottles and two milk bottles were also excavated. Cans were identified as having contained food, condensed milk, tobacco, baby powder, boot polish, and oil. Personal artifacts included a garter, pocket watches and alarm clocks, combs, many buttons, and more than a dozen work boots. Many of the industrial artifacts retrieved were associated with logging, such as saw blades, files, and ax heads.

Portions of at least several stoves were recovered, usually in the presumed location of a residence and from a relatively inexpensive variety of stove. There was one outlier – an expensive stove discovered buried behind the stump of a large tree on the periphery of the site. Reviewing catalogs from the early twentieth century, we could see that most stoves could be purchased in the early 1900s for less than $4.00. The stove found buried on the periphery of the site cost $35.75.

Excavations revealed what many thought to be a large safety pin. At public education exhibits, people frequently say it is a kilt pin. When we excavated it, I was thinking it could be a diaper pin. Shortly after its discovery, I was giving a presentation on the project at the Nikkei National Museum and Cultural Centre, and I took the pin along with some other artifacts to show and discuss. There were about 50 Nikkei in the room, mostly elderly. The unanimous opinion was that this was a woman's shawl pin. There was no doubt. Before we could move on to the next artifact, someone volunteered that not only was this evidence of women at the camp, it was also evidence of a winter occupation. I was thrilled. By the time of the presentation, I was already thinking that perhaps the site continued to be occupied after logging had ceased, but I had no good evidence. Knowing this was considered a winter artifact was good news, supporting the theory of a more permanent occupation at McKenzie Creek. Reports of small-scale logging operations in the region during the early twentieth century usually indicated that the camps were abandoned during winter months. It was too difficult to log in winter. At the end of the presentation at the Nikkei National Museum, a woman approached to show the shawl pin that she was currently wearing, since it was winter. It was identical to the one found at the McKenzie Creek site.

ANOTHER "AH HA" MOMENT

Chapter 5 included a brief description of an "ah ha" moment when, reading a report about another camp, I realized the McKenzie Creek site was unique in the region, with many small houses or cabins, each with a Nikkei logger living with his family. A second "ah ha" moment occurred about a year later. Continuing a deep dive into historical research, I came across a master's thesis on local history published in 1943 (Woodward-Reynolds 1943). The thesis mentions the existence of a lumber mill in the late nineteenth and early twentieth centuries near Rice Lake in

Figure 6.3. Artifacts from the McKenzie Creek Site. Credit: R. Muckle.

the valley, a mill operated by Nikkei who also lived in a camp there. The thesis states, "Many of these families remained on the site until they were evacuated from the area by Federal order in 1942" (Woodward-Reynolds 1943, 87). The mill near Rice Lake is well known and well documented although there is no visible evidence remaining. I asked all the residents who were living in the area and would have walked by Rice Lake on their way to school or work every day in the 1920s and 1930s whether they ever recalled Nikkei living anywhere near the lake. They did not. They were certain no Nikkei lived close by. The "ah ha" moment came when I realized the author of the thesis must have made a mistake. There had not been a mill or camp of Nikkei near Rice Lake since the very early years of the twentieth century. She must have heard of Nikkei living in a camp and assumed it was at Rice Lake, but in reality, it was some distance away at what we now recognize as the McKenzie Creek site. This created another shift in direction for the project. Now a primary objective was to show that the McKenzie Creek site continued to be occupied until the forced evacuation of Nikkei people from the coastal area of the region in 1942. Addressing this objective is discussed in Chapter 7.

ASSESSING SIGNIFICANCE AT MCKENZIE CREEK

The McKenzie Creek site is highly significant.

Scientific significance is assessed as being high because of the uniqueness of the site and is primarily based on its value in learning about the Nikkei experience in the region in the early twentieth century. The site helps us understand how they were living, how they preserved their identity, how they maintained their lives in a largely unknown settlement, and how they prepared for a forced evacuation.

The site's historic and ethnic significance is assessed as being high because the site is associated with Eikichi Kagetsu, a very prominent member of the Nikkei community in Canada, and because it is more broadly a good example of the place of Nikkei in the forestry industry. It is further significant because of its association with the forced evacuation of Nikkei from coastal regions.

The site is assessed as having high public significance too. It is easily accessed, has high archaeological visibility of features that are easy to interpret, and offers the potential for reconstruction or restoration. The assessment is also based on the widespread popular appeal of the site, which the media helped establish, as described in Chapter 7.

The significance of the site is recognized by the provincial government. Detailing the significance of the site and why that significance should be recognized, I nominated the site for inclusion on the Register of Historic Places in British Columbia. The nomination was accepted in 2017. The description of the site in the register is as follows:

> The Seymour Valley in North Vancouver was home to a community of Japanese Canadian families in the early part of the twentieth century. Likely founded by prominent Japanese Canadian and entrepreneur Eikichi Kagetsu, also owner of the Deep Bay Logging Company, the community was initially established as a logging camp about 1920. After its initial use as a logging camp around 1920, the camp likely continued as a residential camp in the forest for a group of Japanese until the WW II internment in 1942. This place is an excellent example of an early twentieth century logging camp, supporting the significant role Japanese Canadians had in the lumber industry. It is the only Japanese camp documented and excavated in the province, providing a glimpse into life in Japanese

logging camps in the early twentieth century. It exhibits evidence of maintaining traditional ways of life (e.g., bathhouse) even in remote areas such as logging camps. It is also an alternative source for understanding the Japanese experience in British Columbia in the early twentieth century.

PUBLIC EDUCATION

Public education associated with the McKenzie Creek site was substantial and diverse. Many K–12 school groups participated in activities at the site, and there were multiple scheduled tours for community groups, including tours for only Nikkei. There were many lectures given to community groups and artifacts from the site were featured in many public exhibits. For three years, we had a blog for the project, which reached thousands of people in dozens of countries with daily updates.

Public education has always been a key component of the project, and the McKenzie Creek site's ease of access and high archaeological visibility made it particularly attractive for many. Overall, we had an average of about 150 visitors to the site each field season, resulting in more than 1,000 visits over the several seasons of fieldwork at the site. Some of these were people simply walking up the pathway and wondering what was going on. Most were prearranged visits for groups.

Knowing that the 2019 field season was likely going to be the last field season at the site, we reached out to many members of the public, encouraging them to visit. We especially contacted those who had expressed an interest in visiting in prior years but whom, for some reason, we could not accommodate.

Some of those we reached out to included local archaeologists, historians, and museum professionals. We also got in touch with journalist Brent Richter. Richter had already written about the Seymour Valley Archaeology Project and had expressed a keen interest in visiting the McKenzie Creek site, but it was difficult, logistically, to make it work. In the final days of fieldwork, as a courtesy and because of his past involvement and expressed interest, I invited Richter to visit, which he accepted. I had no agenda of pitching a story. Richter decided to write a story anyway, and it led to worldwide interest in the project, discussed in the next chapter.

7

Making the Fieldwork Meaningful

Traditionally, most sharing of research knowledge remained within academia, but in recent times it has become expected that research be shared with non-academic audiences and groups so that they may use it for their benefit.

– Muckle and Camp (2021, 77)

INTRODUCTION

There is a common saying in archaeology that goes "For every week in the field, there is a month in the lab." This is a generalization of course, but there is some validity in it. For many archaeologists, fieldwork is the easy part. Making sense of the artifacts and other data collected is often more difficult and time consuming.

Artifacts and descriptions of sites, features, and more on their own are relatively meaningless. It is the task of archaeologists to give the results of fieldwork meaning. This process starts with the creation of a research design before fieldwork even begins, but analysis and interpretation are operationalized after fieldwork too – in the lab or just during time spent thinking.

It is important to make fieldwork meaningful. Excavation is destructive, and without making the research meaningful archaeologists are no better, and a case could be made that they are worse, than anyone else who willfully destroys a known site. Archaeologists are morally, ethically, and, in many cases, legally bound to share their data, which is the most common way of making the research meaningful.

Archaeologists have responsibilities to make their research meaningful to other archaeologists, to funding agencies, to descendant communities, and to the public.

This chapter has four major sections: "Working in the Lab"; "Education"; "Answering Questions, Drawing Inferences"; and "Making the Research Meaningful by Sharing." This chapter first looks at how lab work contributes to adding meaning to archaeology projects, as well as at some of the challenges archaeologists face when classifying artifacts meaningfully. It then considers the significant role of archaeology in the education of students and the public. Next, it discusses archaeology's role not only in contributing directly to our knowledge of the past but also in training us in the ability to ask and answer questions and draw inferences. And finally, the chapter outlines the process of making archaeological research meaningful by sharing results with stakeholders: other archaeologists and heritage researchers, the organizations that supported the research, descendant communities, and the public.

WORKING IN THE LAB

While most projects schedule the bulk of lab work to be completed once excavations are finished, some projects start the lab work while projects are ongoing. Some projects have temporary labs set up at the field sites.

For the Seymour Valley Archaeology Project, we did not have a field lab, but some students did occasionally work with artifacts and other recovered remains on some days while fieldwork was ongoing. It was common for a few students to work in the lab on campus while the majority worked in the field. Students would rotate in and out of lab work.

Capilano University does not have permanent lab space for archaeology, but in some years, we were able to transform an anthropology classroom into lab space; other years, we were able to utilize a proper lab space once belonging to the horticulture program.

In the field, materials for lab analysis, such as artifacts, level bags, and soil samples were all put in separate bags, each labeled with details of provenience and date. Field versions of artifact inventory forms included details of provenience, date, measurements, description, material (e.g., ceramic, glass, metal), presumed function (e.g., lantern glass, rice bowl), and a sketch of the artifact.

Once the materials were in the lab, the first task was to sort them. For example, artifacts were separated from level bags and soil samples. Further, during the initial sort, artifacts were separated into the broad categories of ceramics, glass, metal, and other.

Then artifacts were typically cleaned, and details about each artifact were entered into a permanent catalog. Artifact inventory forms completed in the field were used as a reference, but the entries in the catalog were much more detailed, with more precise measurements and descriptions. Once in the lab, then, students had to take more precise measurements and develop more thorough descriptions of artifacts. Artifacts were also photographed and sometimes drawn. Permanent catalog numbers were written on most artifacts. When multiple fragments of an artifact such as a bowl or bottle were recognized as belonging together, we sometimes refit the pieces. We did not do this for most broken items though. We mostly restricted this treatment to dishes or bowls we thought would be of interest in public displays – both to show how we could refit artifacts from scattered pieces and to better present artifacts that we assumed would have popular appeal, such as sake bottles or rice bowls with artful designs.

Lab work also included sorting material in the level bags. Working with level bags is certainly among the least glamorous jobs in archaeological lab work, but it is valuable. During fieldwork, excavators would typically put into these bags all the pieces of ceramics, glass, and metal that did not meet the criteria of being classified as an artifact for the site. (In order to be classified as an artifact, an item needed to have a diagnostic characteristic that we could learn from, e.g., such as age, function, or manufacturer.) For this project, nails were also put into level bags, thousands of them. The reason nails were not considered artifacts is that there were so many. It would have taken too much time to record them individually. Once sorted, the individual pieces of material were counted and weighed.

During fieldwork, excavators unsure of whether an item was an artifact or not routinely put that item in a level bag, essentially passing the buck on the decision of whether it was an artifact to the person working in the lab. Many small items that were really artifacts, such as buttons, were often recovered from level bags and cataloged as artifacts. This change in classification was primarily because the buttons were so dirty the excavator was not sure whether the item was an artifact or simply a dirt-covered pebble or lump of earth. There were also, however, many small items that excavators thought might be artifacts but were not, such as small rocks covered in dirt.

The Conundrum of Classification and Analysis

Artifacts can be classified and analyzed in multiple ways. The system used for any project is primarily dependent on the project objectives. Generally, archaeologists first make a decision on whether to use a descriptive system, a functional system, or a hybrid of those two. A descriptive system is based on observable and measurable traits such as size, shape, and material. A functional system is based on the presumed function of an artifact, and a hybrid system combines both the descriptive and the functional approaches (using both function and form, e.g., material, shape, and size, to classify an artifact).

Using a functional classification system is common in historical archaeology, so early in the project, when most fieldwork was focused on settler sites, we used a functional system, classifying objects under categories such as saw blade, file, or beer bottle. Once the basic classification was done, we added further descriptive variables, resulting, for example, in such categories as small brown beer bottle.

When we started excavating Japanese artifacts, especially Japanese dishes and bottles, we had to rethink the classification system. Ultimately, we decided to use the classification systems that would be of most use to other archaeologists. For Japanese dishes and bottles, we decided on the same categories as those used by Doug Ross, one of the leading experts in Nikkei sites in North America. Since I was new to historical archaeology in general and fairly ignorant of Asian

Figure 7.1. Working in the Lab. Credit: R. Muckle.

American archaeology, I checked with a few other archaeologists studying Nikkei sites. I knew Doug and was familiar with his work. I assumed his work, including his classification systems, were good, but I wanted to make sure. My correspondence with other archaeologists confirmed it – Ross's work, including his classification systems for dishes and bottles, was recognized as being good and would probably set the standard.

For non-Japanese bottles, we used the U.S. Bureau of Land Management's "Historic Glass Bottle Identification Guide" hosted on the web page of the Society for Historical Archaeology (sha.org).

Metal cans we classified according to the common functional categories used widely in historical archaeology, categories such as food cans and tobacco cans. Food cans were further classified according to function (e.g., for evaporated milk), size, and manufacturing technique (e.g., hole-in-top or sanitary can).

Working in the lab includes using the internet to find similar items to those recovered during excavations. This may lead to discovering the date and place of manufacture of an artifact, as well as its function. Internet research was helpful, for example, in pinpointing details about the tobacco tin pictured in Figure 7.1.

EDUCATION

We think a strong case can be made that the project's fieldwork has been made meaningful through education – it has trained university students in field methods and the culture of archaeology, and it has educated the public.

Many of the 217 students who attended the field school have gone on to careers in archaeology and related fields, such as work in museums and teaching. For a while, there was even a name used widely by archaeologists whose first fieldwork experiences were on the Seymour Valley Archaeology Project. Some more experienced professionals would sometimes refer to them as "Mucklettes." Multiple archaeologists have told me they like hiring crew who have worked on the Seymour Valley Archaeology Project, primarily because of the project's emphasis on the culture of field archaeology, including the importance of having a good work ethic.

We think the fieldwork has been made meaningful by all the public education we have done. We hosted many visits by K–12 school groups whose students observed and participated in fieldwork; we held several public excavation days, gave many public lectures and presentations to community groups, curated dozens of exhibits; and we blogged the project to viewers around the world.

Pictured in Figure 7.2 is one of the many public education displays or exhibits associated with the Seymour Valley Archaeology Project. Public education was a key component of the project.

Linked with the project's public education aim has been its openness to media. Many thousands of people have watched television news and cable TV programming featuring the project or have listened to radio interviews with the project director, who answered "yes" to dozens of interview requests from journalists wishing to write about the project.

ANSWERING QUESTIONS, DRAWING INFERENCES

Of course, to educate means to contribute meaningfully to the public's store of knowledge – knowledge not only about archaeological methods, processes, and artifacts but also about the history and culture of particular places and peoples. So, to be meaningful, this knowledge must be put in context, which requires us to ask good questions about

Figure 7.2. Public Education Display. Credit: R. Muckle.

and draw logical inferences from what we discover. The kinds of questions we asked during the initial design of the project and the project's first years, when we were focusing on the settler sites especially, were relatively easy to answer: Are there any more sites in the homestead area? What is the integrity of the sites? What about the artifacts – what kinds and how many are there? Would there be public interest in this site? What kind of significance do these sites have? Does the archaeology support the stories told in local histories? How can this archaeology contribute to our knowledge of local history?

Here are some of our answers. We found several more sites in the homestead area than are documented in local history. The integrity of the sites in the homestead area is generally good; we found many surface artifacts, but those that were there had little perceived value to the public, historians, or archaeologists. Sites in the homestead area, particularly the Fowler and The Point sites, have high public significance, but moderate scientific, historic, ethnic, or economic significance. The archaeology does indeed support the published histories of the area, and it contributes to the local history of the homestead area by documenting known sites, assessing the integrity of the sites, and adding more sites to the historical record.

As the project proceeded and Nikkei logging sites became a primary focus, the questions began to change. We started to ask more complex questions: How old is this site? How is this site organized? Was this site occupied by a mixed group including Nikkei or by only Nikkei? What was the probable population at the site? What was the ratio of males to females? Is there evidence of children?

For the Suicide Creek site, the answers are as follows. The site was probably occupied for a few years in the early 1920s. This is supported by the dating of artifacts and the knowledge that Eikichi Kagetsu moved his operations out of the Seymour Valley around this time. Trees growing over features also suggest an abandonment of at least several decades. The site was organized as a typical small-scale logging camp in the Pacific Northwest, with a bunkhouse and communal cooking and eating areas. The artifact assemblage (e.g., the dishes) and many of the bottles (both alcohol and pharmaceutical) are Japanese, suggesting an all-Nikkei occupation. The number of people living at the site was probably about 20–30, including one woman or a few women who likely cooked and cleaned. There is no evidence of children at Suicide Creek.

For the McKenzie Creek site, the answers are different. The site was probably initially established sometime in the period of 1918–20 and used for a few years as a logging camp. Following this period, Kagetsu probably moved the workers from the McKenzie Creek site to the camp at Suicide Creek to log that area for a few years before he moved his logging operations out of the valley. It is reasonable to think that while the loggers were at the Suicide Creek site, their families stayed behind at the McKenzie Creek site. When Kagetsu decided to leave the Seymour Valley, some of the Nikkei loggers likely decided to remain, living with their families at the McKenzie Creek site, where they stayed until the forced evacuation of Nikkei from coastal regions in 1942. The population at the McKenzie Creek site was probably about 50. This is based on the identification of 14 cabins or small houses, which we assume housed three to four people per residence. The population was likely all Nikkei, and there were likely children living with their parents.

Preliminary dating of artifacts cannot be used to support with certainty an occupation of the site up to 1942. No artifact can be dated with certainty to the post-1920 period. There are, however, Japanese ceramic dishes with "Made in Japan" written on them, a practice which only became widespread beginning in 1920. Manufacturing techniques for cans and bottles can often be used to determine the approximate age of an item, but we can't use them to date the site to post-1920 with certainty. Many of the bottles and cans, for example, are made with techniques that were used in the 1930s, but these methods were also used in the 1920s and earlier.

The biggest question for the project in the most recent years has been whether, after Nikkei-controlled logging in the area ceased in the early 1920s, a group of Nikkei continued to live there until 1942. The following section addresses this topic.

Was the McKenzie Creek Site a Secret Settlement?

As described in Chapter 6, a master's thesis published in 1943 mentions that Nikkei continued to live at a camp in the Seymour Valley until their forced removal in 1942. I believe that camp is the McKenzie Creek site. Evidence is largely circumstantial, but substantive.

One line of evidence in support of an ongoing occupation of the site is the apparent hiding of objects. It is well known that, in preparation for their forced removal from the coastal areas, many Nikkei hid objects. The expensive cookstove buried behind a tree was almost certainly hidden. It had a value of approximately 10 times the other stoves, which were left in the residences.

Another object that was likely hidden was the camera found in the excavation of the bathhouse. Cameras would not have been allowed in the internment camps, so this one was probably hidden in the bathhouse.

Another line of evidence to support the theory that Nikkei lived at McKenzie Creek until their forced removal in 1942 is the very high proportion of personal items left at the site. Compared, for example, to the Suicide Creek site, the McKenzie Creek site had a much higher proportion of personal items. At the McKenzie Creek site, we found several timepieces (alarm clocks and pocket watches), several toothbrushes, a garter, gaming pieces, a ceramic foot warmer, combs, and more. We also found many buttons and more than a dozen work boots. This makes sense when we consider that Nikkei were allowed to bring only a minimal number of things with them during the evacuation (e.g., one or two suitcases).

We also found a much higher proportion of household items than one would normally expect if the site had been abandoned in a normal way. These items included dishes. When we compared the dishes at the McKenzie Creek site with those at the Suicide Creek site, we observed that many of them were of the same kind, with the same designs. Yet the dishes at the Suicide Creek site were more fragmented, probably broken and recognized as trash before the site was even abandoned. The dishes at the McKenzie Creek site, on the other hand, were in much better condition. Many of them were complete, and some had only minor chips. Many of the dishes were evidently in useable condition when the site was abandoned.

The fact that many of the household and personal items, such as dishes, lanterns, and clothing, were found in clusters representing the locations of residences, rather than in middens, further supports the idea that the Nikkei remained at the site until forced to relocate. It appears that the residents simply packed what they deemed most essential and walked out of their residences, leaving all the remaining household items in situ (in place).

Yet another line of evidence supporting an ongoing occupation of the McKenzie Creek site after the logging had ceased is the presence of a solid cedar plank road running through the site. Using cedar plank roads in the study area was common, but when a logging company finished logging an area, it usually took the planks away. The planks had value. They could be used again. Although we can identify the location of plank roads running hundreds of meters to and from the site, almost all of the planks have long been removed from these roads. The plank road *within* the site, however, remains intact. Presumably the planks comprising the roads around the site were removed, but the plank road within the site was left for the use of the residents, as a kind of boardwalk.

MAKING THE RESEARCH MEANINGFUL BY SHARING

Research is made meaningful by sharing – sharing it with archaeologists and other heritage professionals, with the organizations that funded the research, with descendant communities, and with the public.

Sharing with Archaeologists and Other Heritage Professionals

Sharing with archaeologists and historians was done in many ways. Presentations on the project were given at many conferences, including those held by the American Anthropological Association, *BC Studies*, the Canadian Archaeological Association, the Canadian Historical Association, the Society for American Archaeology, and the World Archaeological Congress. Several reports on the project appeared in *The Midden*, a periodical of the Archaeological Society of British Columbia, and an article was written for the British Columbia Association of Professional Archaeologists. Scholarly articles appeared in *BC Studies* (Muckle 2017) and the *International Journal of Historical Archaeology* (Muckle 2021). Site tours were given to approximately 100 students participating in archaeology field schools with other universities, to about 30 archaeology graduate and postdoctoral students, and to 20 practicing archaeologists from other local universities or from the world of commercial archaeology. Multiple invitations were accepted to present on the project to audiences of archaeology students and professors at other universities.

It is through sharing with archaeologists and others in related fields that progress is made, both in our understanding of the human past and in our knowledge of archaeological method and theory. Archaeologists and other heritage professionals may compare the results of this project with other findings and build on the project's research, whether that research has to do with local history, the archaeology of logging camps, the Japanese diaspora, or something else.

Sharing with Organizations That Funded the Research

The Seymour Valley Archaeology Project operated with the support of both Capilano University and the Metro Vancouver Regional District. Progress reports on the project were made to the university in both written and verbal forms and included multiple presentations to the university board and public presentations organized by the university. The results have also been shared with Metro Vancouver, which can use the information in its planning of future educational and research initiatives as well as in its land management and heritage resource plans.

BOX 7.1 THE MEDIA IS CRAZY

There has always been some media interest in the project over its duration, but things got pretty crazy as the project started winding down.

Knowing the fieldwork was coming to a close, I contacted a local journalist – Brent Richter of the *North Shore News* – to see if he would like to come for a site visit. It was the last week of the last season of fieldwork. The *North Shore News* had published multiple stories on the project, including a recent one. Richter had expressed much interest in the project and had wanted to come to the site previously, but I just couldn't make it work logistically. So, as a courtesy, I invited him to the site during the last days of excavation. I was not inviting him to get media attention. It was simply a courtesy. I wasn't expecting him to write a story, but he did, and it took the project to previously unimagined heights of national and international media attention. It was crazy.

Richter wrote a feature-length story, which later won top prize for the best newspaper story with a historical theme published in British Columbia and the Yukon. It was a very good article.

A few days after Richter's story broke, I got a call from a popular journalist and radio personality on one of the top-rated radio programs in Metro Vancouver. Gloria Macarenko of the CBC's *On the Coast* program had read the article, and she thought it had broad appeal. So she invited me on the program that afternoon, live, in the studio. The interview went well, and Macarenko suggested there would likely be interest from the news division.

A few days later, the CBC's online news service published a story, and then things really got crazy. In short order, I was contacted by media from around the world for interviews. One of the first to call for an interview was a journalist writing for the *Smithsonian Magazine*. The magazine published a story about the project in 2019, which, in 2020, was declared the top archaeology story of 2019.

Archaeology Magazine had a couple of issues containing reports on the project. *Atlas Obscura* published a story. Friends and colleagues were telling me there were stories about the project on Reddit, Apple News, MSN, Google News, and Boredomtherapy.com. Stacker.com described it as one of the greatest archaeological discoveries of all time (Sweet 2020), right up there with Tutankhamen's tomb and Machu Picchu (which is ridiculous, but the story was republished in some major US newspapers). In Canada, the *National Post* published a story in its national edition, which was also republished in some local papers in the same newspaper group, such as the *Vancouver Sun* and *The Province*.

A couple of days after the original article on the project by Brent Richter was published, he sent me a message telling me the project was becoming very popular in Japan. Links to his story had already been retweeted thousands of times. The story was eventually translated into Japanese by another media service. The chief of the North American bureau for a large Japanese newspaper flew from New York to spend a day at the site and in the lab, which led to two stories in that Japanese newspaper. *Newsweek Japan* did a story. A government agency in Japan did a story on the project. Someone sent me a copy of a magazine article on the project written in Estonian. There was another in French.

I was interviewed live on a BBC radio program from the United Kingdom. The radio host repeatedly said how fascinating the project was. I was a bit surprised to hear this from someone who was living in the land of Stonehenge, Vikings, Roman ruins, castles, and more.

After the initial stories were published by mainstream media outlets and popular magazines, they started hitting some niche markets. An automotive publication linked a story to information about my own personal truck, used to transport equipment to the site. A beer publication focused on the beer bottles.

Most of the project members' experiences with the media were positive. The average length of the interviews I gave to journalists from mainstream media outlets or popular magazines was 45 minutes. They wanted to make sure they got things right. And, for the most part, they did.

Some of the media stories were disconcerting. Many stories appearing on the internet were heavily plagiarized from material published in the mainstream media or popular press, without proper reference. Some stories about the project were used as click bait. Clicking on one headline about the project led to a hate site. The project even entered the realm of fake news – an article used photos of the site, artifacts from other projects that had been depicted in various publications, and a few basic facts about these projects and wound the lot into a ridiculous story, placing our site in the United States and involving lost temples and mythological figures.

The craziness of the media began in 2019 and extended through 2021. I had been working at the McKenzie Creek site off and on for 15 years, and I'd had the basic story worked out for 12. So for over a decade, I had told the same basic story – how the McKenzie Creek site was established as a logging camp and used for a few years around 1920, after which it very likely transitioned to a more permanent and somewhat secret settlement for the use of Nikkei until the forced removal of Nikkei in 1942. We had done much more research, but the story remained the same.

The story had been told many times – in published news stories, in presentations to the public and to other archaeologists and historians, in numerous articles and reports. There had even been interviews on the radio, but the story had never before received more than local interest.

While the story remained the same, the world, apparently, changed. What was of little or no interest prior to 2019 suddenly became a major story, garnering local, national, and international attention.

Sharing with Descendant Communities

The research has been shared with the Nikkei community. The project director wrote multiple articles for *Nikkei Images*, a periodical of the Nikkei community, organized multiple site tours specifically for members of the Nikkei community, and delivered multiple presentations at the Nikkei National Museum and Cultural Centre. The collected artifacts have also been shared with the Nikkei community (see Chapter 8).

Sharing with the Public

Sharing with the public is described in multiple previous chapters. Overall, many thousands of people have been able visit the sites and exhibits, participate in excavations, listen to lectures, and read blogs. The project director has written a few articles on the project for a public interested in history (e.g., Muckle 2020a).

Members of the public have also been able to read and listen to media reports about the project, which have introduced it to hundreds of thousands or more people. Figure 7.3 illustrates the trajectory of media interest in the project in 2019 and 2020, starting with the Richter story on the project in a local newspaper, which led to a radio interview and an article by an online news service. After that, the story of the project really took off, entering into mainstream media, archaeology-focused magazines, niche media, and, ultimately, the world of click bait.

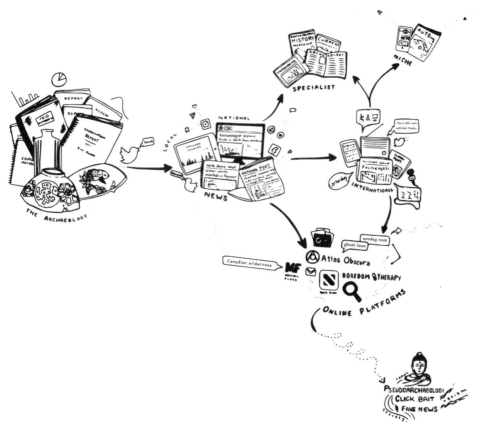

Figure 7.3. The Trajectory of Media Interest. Credit: K. Cook.

8

Endings

Archaeology is never having to say you're finished.
– Dr. Julia King, archaeologist

INTRODUCTION

Excavations stop, laboratory work ceases, reports and articles are written, and archaeologists move on to other things. But projects live on. Other archaeologists may return to the site to carry on further excavations. Artifacts collected but not fully studied may be examined by future archaeologists or archaeology students or become part of museum exhibits. Future archaeologists may wish to classify the artifacts in a different way to work toward different research objectives, answer different questions, test different hypotheses. Field and lab methods may be critiqued. Data will be compared with data from other sites. Interpretations may be reexamined. The best techniques and interpretations used during some project years may not be the best going forward. Everything is up for reconsideration and critique. The project may officially close, but the artifacts, the data, interpretations, reports, articles, and media stories live on.

This chapter brings both the project and the book to a close. It discusses the logistics of closing a project down. It describes what happens to the artifacts and project records and how to plan for future work that might be associated with the project, and it offers some reflections on the Seymour Valley Archaeology Project while detailing some key things that I hope readers will remember. The chapter also includes a box on some hard truths about archaeology.

CLOSING THE PROJECT DOWN: LOGISTICS

In 2019, it was decided to close the project down. The 2019 field season would be the last. The amount of data being collected was becoming overwhelming. We needed to stop collecting information and start spending more time working with it, making sense of it, interpreting it, and sharing it. We had been doing these things in bits for years, but it was really time to get more control. We can't collect data forever. The site began with a commitment to one field season only and involved a total of 15 students and no collection of artifacts. We were now in season 14 – with close to 3,000 artifacts recorded over the years by more than 200 field school students. We needed to stop. We needed time for more analysis, thinking, and report writing.

It was mentally tough, closing down the project. The project director loved all aspects of the project, students enjoyed it, and it had the support of the university, Metro Vancouver, and local communities. But it was time. How much fieldwork was enough? We weren't sure but felt we had done enough. It was time to move on.

Knowing in the summer of 2019 that we were unlikely to restart excavations, we paid special attention to our last days in the field. It was a bit different from previous seasons when we knew we would be back the next year. We backfilled the units as usual, but this time we also replanted vegetation on some of the units. There was a little bit more sadness than usual when we backfilled, removed the shelters, and did the final walk-around to make sure we weren't leaving anything behind.

Once we left the field, issues arose that we had thought about but had never before had to deal with directly – what happens to the artifacts and project records?

The initial agreement between the university and Metro Vancouver was that Metro Vancouver would retain ownership of the artifacts but they would remain in the possession of the anthropology department at Capilano University until the end of the project.

Capilano University is a teaching-focused university with no facilities for the proper storage of artifacts. I proposed to Metro Vancouver that we ask both the Nikkei National Museum and MONOVA (the Museum of North Vancouver) about taking some of the artifacts for their permanent collections. Curators and others from both museums had visited the excavations in 2019 so had an idea of the kinds of artifacts and the context of the artifacts. Both museums responded that, indeed, they would like some of the artifacts.

Following the final season of fieldwork in 2019, we arranged a day in which the curators and other associated professionals from each museum, a representative of Metro Vancouver, and I could meet to facilitate the sharing of artifacts. On the day of the meeting, I brought out all the artifacts of potential interest to the museums, and the representatives from each museum selected the artifacts that museum would like, with the understanding that I would keep them to get all the information I wanted from the artifacts before formally turning them over. In 2020, the artifacts were turned over to each museum, and formal documents transferring ownership to each museum were made.

The Nikkei National Museum and Cultural Centre created an exhibit of some of the artifacts almost immediately in 2020 (Figure 8.1). MONOVA created an exhibit using some of the artifacts in 2021.

I feel immense satisfaction that the project's artifacts went to these two museums. The artifacts are a tangible part of the history of the region and the Nikkei community, and both museums have exhibited enormous support for the project. Some researchers express a preference for keeping an artifact collection together, but, in this case, having artifacts at these two museums, which serve the interests of different groups, is ideal.

It is very rewarding to know that some artifacts from the McKenzie Creek site are now in the collections of and on exhibit at the Nikkei National Museum. Lisa Uyeda, collections manager at the Nikkei National Museum mentioned the artifacts' significance: "If these items are from when the community was forced to leave, it is important now to

Figure 8.1. Artifacts from Nikkei Sites in the Study Area on Display in the Nikkei National Museum, 2021. Credit: Nikkei National Museum and Cultural Centre.

preserve them so they are not lost twice" (Uyeda, personal communication, 2019).

The two museums did not take all the artifacts. Ultimately, each artifact will go to one of five places. Some of the artifacts not going to the museums will be retained by the anthropology department at Capilano University to become part of the teaching collection; some artifacts will be returned to the sites from which they came; and the remainder will be held in proper and accessible storage by Metro Vancouver.

An agreement has been reached that the project records will go to the Archives of North Vancouver, which is part of MONOVA. These records will include many of the documents associated with the project including maps, inventories, reports, agreements, photos, and field notes.

FUTURE WORK ASSOCIATED WITH THE PROJECT

While the fieldwork has ended, and in many ways the project has come to an official end, the project lives on in a kind of unofficial way. The project director plans on continuing to work with collected data for years to come. This includes spending more time on artifact analysis and writing technical reports on the artifacts and features discovered at both the Suicide Creek and McKenzie Creek sites. The project director also plans on continuing to monitor each of the sites investigated.

REFLECTIONS

There are many things about the project to reflect on, mostly positive. One is contributing to the education and experiences of the 217 field school students, many of whom have gone on to careers in archaeology. Other positive reflections include making contributions to local history and archaeology.

Even though it was never the plan to work on Nikkei sites, it was fantastic to make important contributions. In an overview of the history of Japanese diaspora studies, Ross (2021) describes the Seymour Valley Archaeology Project as "[a]mong the earliest and most sustained research initiatives on pre-War Japanese sites" and goes on to note that

BOX 8.1 SOME HARD TRUTHS ABOUT FIELDWORK

For many, the initial appeal of archaeological fieldwork (as outlined in Box 3.1) never wears off. There are many who have long careers as field archaeologists, continuing to enjoy all that it brings. Those who tire of the culture of field archaeology are often able to move into other roles: working in archaeological laboratories, for example, or teaching or doing archaeology-related office work, such as writing reports. Others leave archaeology completely.

People leave archaeological fieldwork for many reasons. Some get tired of the hard truths about field archaeology, which may vary by region and circumstance but generally include working in inclement weather, working in dangerous situations, spending much time away from home, precarious employment, and, in some areas, low wages.

What drives many away is the wear and tear on the body – bushwhacking, hiking, bending, leaping, kneeling, shoveling, lifting, jumping. This is often appealing, or at least manageable, when one is a young adult, but as one gets older, it leads some to find another career.

Jane Luke, a friend of the project director, explains why she left a career in archaeology: "Trowelling in an icy cold test pit ... covered in mud, finding nothing for the 26th day in a row, wearing crappy wet shoes because a bear stole one of my work boots, and mumbling to my coworker 'Shit, girl. We should have gone to law school.'" Jane is now a lawyer.

Some love the life but find it difficult to juggle field archaeology and family. Former field school student Casey McLaughlin, who was a student of the field school and worked on other projects before moving into the world of museums and motherhood, explained, "It is very difficult to be pregnant and do fieldwork...." It is certainly the case, however, that many archaeologists continue to do fieldwork while pregnant and after having taken on childcare responsibilities.

Although addressed in recent years, problems related to the culture of field archaeology have made the profession unattractive to some. Working in the field has been associated with a drinking culture and instances of sexual harassment and abuse, and fieldwork is not very accommodating to people with disabilities and has offered little ethnic diversity, having been dominated by light-skinned people with European ancestry.

One of the objectives of the field school component of the Seymour Valley Archaeology Project was to familiarize students with the culture of archaeological fieldwork. Two things were made clear, although not all projects operate the same way: (i) it is never okay to pressure someone to drink alcohol, and (ii) sexual harassment or abuse is never acceptable.

Another hard truth is that not everyone likes archaeologists. Pothunters often aren't pleased when you don't tell them where the sites with bottles are. During the 2019 field season, there was a guy who regularly rode by the site on a bike, wearing nothing but a bikini type bathing suit. We dubbed him "Naked guy on bike with bikini." He regularly swore at us as he went by. He clearly did not like archaeologists.

Despite the hardships of working in the field, many archaeologists find it to be an extremely fulfilling and rewarding profession. A career in archaeology often presents choices. Those who want to focus on fieldwork can often find work looking for and excavating sites; those who wish to balance fieldwork with lab or office work can often accomplish that, and those who wish to stay in the profession without enduring any of the hardships of fieldwork can also be accommodated as well, working in offices of archaeology-related companies, doing work in heritage-related industries, or teaching.

the project marked "a watershed in the emergence of Japanese diaspora archaeology as a distinct field of study" (596–97).

There are many things we did right with the project. Choosing good students, collaborating, consulting, focusing on public education, incorporating assessments of significance into the fieldwork, transferring ownership of artifacts to museums, and almost always responding to media requests with a "yes" are among them.

We have many good memories of the project – of making discoveries in the ground, of course, but also of working with all the good people associated with the project: visitors to the site, people at public meetings, staff in the LSCR, those associated with museums, and so many more. It was also fantastic watching the formation of social bonds among students working alongside each other during fieldwork. Archaeology is well known for encouraging strong social bonds. On the Seymour Valley Archaeology Project, these social bonds among students led to two marriages.

THINGS TO REMEMBER

There are six important things I hope readers will remember about archaeology in general and the Seymour Valley Archaeology Project in particular.

The first is that *archaeology is not the only way to study the human past.* Archaeology focuses on the physical remains of human activities and is mostly based on science. Other ways of studying the human past include history, both written and oral. Archaeology is not necessarily better than other ways of studying the past, but neither is it worse. As is shown in this book, archaeology complements historical research, fills in gaps of knowledge and understanding, and can offer a more complete, and physical, record.

A second important point to remember is that *the archaeology described in this book is not the only way to do archaeology.* Archaeology is a lens and a framework. But within that framework, there are many alternatives, including alternatives in how to look for sites, how to excavate sites, and how to classify objects. This book provides an example of *one* archaeology project. One hundred archaeologists could have come up with 100 different research designs for this project. And they could all be valid.

The third important thing is that *finding and collecting artifacts is not the end game in archaeology.* Many people, fuelled by media and popular culture, believe that the finding and collecting of artifacts is the primary objective. It is not. Artifacts are important, but they are only one source of data archaeologists use in their research. Finding and collecting artifacts are often the easiest parts of the research process. It is what we can learn from the artifacts that is key. In this regard, in terms of what it can teach us, a broken bottle or a fragment of a dish may be just as important as a complete bottle or dish.

The fourth thing to remember is that this project or *any archaeology project merely provides a snapshot*. The Seymour Valley Archaeology Project focuses on early twentieth century life in what is now the Lower Seymour Conservation Reserve. It is not comprehensive. There are many more known and unknown sites that remain undocumented. More than 95 per cent of the valley remains unexamined by archaeologists.

The fifth important thing is that *archaeology is rarely like its depictions in popular culture*. Archaeology in general and fieldwork in particular can be appealing, but it isn't for everyone. (See Box 8.1.)

The sixth important thing to remember is that *archaeology has value*. It can get people interested in the past, provide a more complete record of the human past, help us better understand and explain the human past, and provide tangible links to that past.

Key Resources and Suggested Readings

For those wishing to delve further into some of the topics or themes discussed in this book, this section provides some key resources and suggested readings.

ON THE CULTURE OF FIELD ARCHAEOLOGY

There is surprisingly little written on the culture of field archaeology. A book edited by Edgeworth (2006) includes several chapters on the ethnography of archaeology projects.

Camp (2019) skillfully weaves scholarship on feminism and archaeology with a personal narrative of her own experience. Voss (2021) provides an overview of harassment. Klehm, Eifling, and Peixotto (2021) are editors of a special issue of *Advances in Archaeological Practice* on the topic of "Health and Wellness in Archaeology." Leighton (2020) discusses issues related to both crossing boundaries between professionalism and friendship and the drinking culture associated with archaeology.

LOCAL HISTORY

Roy (2003) provides an overview of Nikkei in British Columbia during the early twentieth century. The scholarly journal *BC Studies* includes many articles on Nikkei history in the province, including a special issue edited by Geiger (2017).

ARCHAEOLOGY IN BRITISH COLUMBIA

The Midden is a semi-scholarly periodical of the Archaeological Society of British Columbia, which often includes reports and articles on archaeology in the province. Articles on British Columbia can also be found in *BC Studies* and in many of the well-known scholarly archaeology journals such as *American Antiquity* and the *Canadian Journal of Archaeology*.

THE ARCHAEOLOGY OF JAPANESE IN NORTH AMERICA

Camp (2021), Lau-Ozawa and Ross (2021), and Ross (2021) provide overviews of the future, present, and past of the archaeology of the Japanese diaspora, focusing on North America.

ARCHAEOLOGICAL METHODS

Muckle and Camp (2021) is a basic introductory text for archaeology. Baxter (2017) offers a guide for archaeology field schools.

ETHICS

Muckle (2020b) provides an overview of ethics in archaeological fieldwork.

Most professional organizations have codes of ethics, statements of ethics, codes of conduct, or something similar on their websites. Students are directed to the websites of the Register of Professional Archaeologists, the Canadian Archaeological Association, the Society for American Archaeology, and the Society for Historical Archaeology.

MAINSTREAM AND POPULAR ARTICLES ON THE PROJECT

Articles on the Seymour Valley Archaeology Project have appeared in at least several dozen places and have been widely shared via social media. The newspaper article by Richter (2019) is particularly good and kicked off global interest in the project in 2019. This article was shared on Japanese Twitter thousands of times. The article by Katz (2019) published in the *Smithsonian Magazine* was both the most popular article in the magazine for that year and voted the year's top story. The article by Gattuso (2019) in *Atlas Obscura* was also very popular. In addition to writing a couple of scholarly articles on the project (Muckle 2017, 2021), the author also wrote an article for a popular history magazine – *British Columbia History* (Muckle 2020a).

Appendix 1: Field School Students

2000: Jordan Addison, Sean Blanchard, Shannon Gregg, Ryan Jamieson, Cathy Johnson, Eric Lock, James Martin, Casey McLaughlin, Tanya McMaster, Jacqueline Nelsen, Denise Pace, Michelle Poulsen, Cristy Power, Laura Prouse, Alexandra Walsh

2001: Michelle Beatch, Andy Behm, Val Campbell, Magdalena Carrasco, Angela Clarke, Jessen Dakin, Louise Golasovsky, Marcel Koller, Edwin Lee, Devin Manky, Stephanie Martel, Meghan McLeod, Chris Rowe, Victor Sherwood, Tara Thomas

2002: Kimberly Biddlecombe, Caroline Bilesky, Cohen Brown, Hillary Bullock, Jason Bunbury, Sarah Ezer, Charline Ferlatte, Kris Hetherington, Anne Johnson, Geoff McDonald, Marlei McOuatt, Ryan Ogilvie, Meridith Sayer, Michael Wilkinson, Tracy Worner

2003: Jody Dalton, Sue Duxbury, Natasha Fountain, Megan Harvey, Rory Kirkham, Quinton Lee, Elizabeth McLaughlin, Tyler Nesbit, Thomas Pickett, Stacie Pilot, Sean Roberts, Olivia Rosati, Jon Sheppard, Angelina Smith, Dave White, Julie Wright

2004: Craig Boyko, Jason Brawn, Michelle Delaplace, Annie Dumitrescu, Danielle Fancher, Sheriff Hossain, Karla Kloepper, Cleo Legge, Alexa Love, Jennifer Morton, Jean-Paul Salley, Nadia Santoro, Erin Smith, Chris Springer, Emily Wall

2005: Ashley Bangsund, Joseph Cooke, Clayton Fox, Michael Fox, Alison Gares, Lisa Gillis, Beth Henderson, Mykol Knighton,

Sabrina Marchand, James Morfopoulos, Alison Murray, Vickie Pavlovic, Richelle Pittman, Jane Sawyer, Carmen White

2006: Erik Blair, Brittany Carlsen, Allison Dean, Arlette Hernandez, Brittany Hunter, Christina Kwong, Suofei Li, Kate Moloughney, Cam Sherk, Morgan Taylor, Jesse Tucker, Celia Utley, Nigel Washburn, Athena Wong

2007: Bahram Farzady, Lin Guenther, Spencer Kitson, Olga Liberchuk, Ashley Lose-Frahn, Heather Mason, Edmond Ng, Nick Orr, Ines Ortner, Chiara Poscente, Crystal Sawyer, Robin Smith, Anna Stewart, Cassandra Wilson

2008: Erin Baldwin, Boris Bozic, Nicholas Chesworth, Mike Coutts, Nyla Dougan, Shane Garstin, Alexa Gygax, Tyler Hicks, Kristy Kinshela, Alex Lee, Sean MacLaren, Kim Meyer, Eric Orr, Bev Rapley, Kaylah Zander

2009: Andrei Axenov, Devon de Balsi-Brown, Elaine Einarson, Shannon Gahan, Nicole Harrison, Asja Hot, Sandy Keim, Christie Leung, Camille Nouellet, Keenan Parker, Eiler Pedersen, Kaylen Riedlinger, Cam Shields, Almira Walde-Renaud

2010: Brittany Allinson, Sean Barnes, Boris Bora Guc, Jessica Clayton, Simon Danvers, Suzannah Forbes, Andrea Goutier, Max Meredith, Anja Micevic, Nadia Pucci, Sonya Reid, Paul Roote, Verena Schneider, Rikki Seddon, Andy Tung

2012: Lindsay Flynn, Alexis Forsyth, Mark Galvani, Evan Guiton, Willow Hunt-Scott, Nathan Laronde, Sarah McKenny, Rebecca McKenzie, Andrew McManus, Kitty Mork, Spencer Mulder, Ryan Pugh, Dini Stamatopulous, Jasmin Sykes, Meghan Walley

2013: Kelsey Bates, Richard Bruce, Kathleen Cottrell, Nathan Daigle, Wendy Dallian, Erin Dunlop, Emma Kimm-Jones, Jeneva Ledding, Tiana Lewis, Caitlin Manz, Ananda Noseworthy, Nadine Ryan, Cameron Van Hemmen, Amanda Vick

2019: Shaunti Bains, Rohan Beynon-Mackinnon, Aza Bryson, Fazila Buksh, Alyssa Calvin, Ali Casey, Mitch Day, Harmanpreet Kaur, Kirsten Larson, Allyah Lewis, Meredith Miller, Phoenix Monro, Karoline Moore, Siobhan Parker, Sepideh Sadeghi, Nikki Simon, Angus Thomson

Appendix 2: Assessing Site Significance

Assessing the significance of an archaeological site is a common activity for archaeologists, especially when doing commercial archaeology. Because the work undertaken by the Seymour Valley Archaeology Project has value for the Metro Vancouver Regional District, including for making informed decisions about activities that could potentially impact areas close to the site locations, assessing significance was included in the project's activities. This appendix describes the kinds of significance archaeologists working in British Columbia are expected to consider, and it lists the criteria used to assess significance. Assessing a site's significance may be different in other regions. The information here is extracted from the British Columbia Archaeology Branch's "Impact Assessment Guidelines," available on the Archaeology Branch's website.

Scientific Significance: This refers to the potential of the site to contribute to understanding human history or to address archaeological research problems.

Historic Significance: Specifically for historic period archaeological sites, historic significance relates to how the site may be associated with settlement, land use, exploration, historic events, figures, groups, and organizations.

Public Significance: This refers to the potential for a site to contribute to an understanding of the past by the public. Things to consider

include the presence of easily visible and interpretable features, the
site's ease of access, and its uniqueness.

Ethnic Significance: This refers to sites having significance in relation
to a particular ethnic group.

Economic Significance: Sites may be assessed based on their having
some economic or monetary value, such as the potential of charging
a fee to visit the site.

On a very simple scale, sites may be described as being of "low," "medium," or "high" significance for each kind of significance. It is common,
however, to use a five-point scale of "low," "low-medium," "medium,"
"medium-high," and "high." Assessments include considerations of site
integrity, which is a measure of how much the site has been disturbed or
otherwise altered. If the integrity of the site has been compromised, the
site rarely has high significance.

Glossary

academic archaeology Archaeology based out of colleges, universities, and museums. Academic archaeology projects are usually driven by pure research interests (compared, for example, to *commercial archaeology* projects, which are driven mostly by averting the unnecessary destruction of archaeological sites by development projects).

arbitrary levels Predetermined levels, such as every 5 cm, at which archaeologists excavate. At the end of every 5 cm level, archaeologists make notes and record all the finds discovered within that level. Compare *natural levels.*

archaeological impact assessment A kind of archaeology that is commonly done in advance of development projects. During these assessments, archaeologists determine the potential impact of a project on archaeological sites.

archaeological site Any location where there is physical evidence of human activity.

archaeological visibility The degree to which the physical remains of human activity, such as sites, features, and artifacts, are visible. This visibility is usually assessed on a scale from "low archaeological visibility," which means the remains are difficult to see, to "high archaeological visibility," which means the remains are easy to see.

archaeology The study of humans through the things they have left behind, such as sites, features, and artifacts. Primarily, archaeologists study the tangible, physical evidence of human activities.

artifacts   Portable objects manufactured or utilized by people. In the LSCR, artifacts include, for example, dishes, bottles, tools, nails, buttons, stoves, lanterns, and coins. Sometimes artifacts are known as "belongings."

Asian American archaeology   Archaeology focusing on the activities of people of Asian descent in North America. Most commonly, this archaeology concerns those with ancestry in China or Japan.

backfilling   Putting the dirt, or backfill, back in the excavation units.

British Columbia Heritage Conservation Act   The legislation protecting archaeological sites in the province of British Columbia.

cedar plank road   A solid wood road constructed of thick cedar planks laid side by side. Such roads were commonly used in the LSCR for hauling sleds loaded with *shingle bolts*.

Coast Salish   Dozens of distinct Indigenous groups and peoples (First Nations and Native Americans) whose territories lie in the southwest portion of British Columbia and the northwest portion of Washington State.

collaborative archaeology   Archaeologists working with other organizations or groups, such as descendant communities or other agencies. The Seymour Valley Archaeological Project involved a collaborative arrangement between Capilano University and the Metro Vancouver Regional District.

commercial archaeology   Archaeology done by contract, usually in advance of development projects. This archaeology is also called "cultural resource management (CRM)" or "consulting arch." Commercial archaeologists often do an *archaeological impact assessment*.

community archaeology   Archaeology done in association with or for the benefit of communities. These communities may be local and based on geography (such as a neighborhood), or they may be formed from a group of people with something else in common, such as a school group or a *descendant community*.

cultural resource management (CRM)   See *commercial archaeology*.

culture history   The sequence of events in an area.

curation crisis   The situation of having more artifacts than can be properly stored and maintained.

descendant community   Usually refers to the group of people living today who can trace their ancestry to the group of people being studied. Direct genealogical links are not necessary.

draft horse   A horse from one of several large breeds of horses used primarily for work, such as for pulling things.

Euro-Canadian   Adjective referring to Canadians of European descent, who are sometimes called "settlers" or "Whites."

features   Non-portable objects manufactured or modified by people. Examples include houses and other buildings, fences, trails, roads, ditches, and gardens.

GPS   Global positioning system.

ground-truth   Finding physical evidence on or in the ground of activity. In archaeology, ground-truthing may refer to searching for and finding evidence of activities that were widely thought or known to have occurred, but for which there was no physical evidence. Ground-truthing may also refer to verifying suspected sites based on remote sensing techniques.

historical archaeology   Archaeology that focuses on a time period for which written records of the area also exist. The Seymour Valley Archaeology Project is an example of historical archaeology.

industrial archaeology   Archaeology focused on industrial activities, such as logging and mining.

in situ   In place. The term describes something, such an artifact or feature, found in place, in other words, in its original context.

Japanese Canadian   See *Nikkei*.

Japanese diaspora   The spread of Japanese people from Japan to the rest of the world.

judgmental sampling   A kind of sampling that is biased by an investigator's objectives, experience, or opinion. See also *nonjudgmental sampling*.

level bags   Bags to collect non-artifactual material while excavating a level in an archaeological site. What is collected may include undiagnostic cultural material. If archaeologists think an object might be an artifact but are not certain, they might put it in a level bag for further analysis in the lab.

Lillooet Trail   A trail constructed in the late 1800s to move cattle from the interior of the province, near Lillooet, to the Vancouver area. The trail is widely considered to have been a failure, constructed at enormous cost, but with poor results. Some reports suggest it was never used; others say it was used once. Part of the trail went through what is now the LSCR.

logistics   The organizational details. For archaeology, logistics usually includes such things as obtaining permits and permissions, arranging travel and accommodation, obtaining equipment and supplies, and hiring crew.

Lower Seymour Conservation Reserve (LSCR)   A 5,668-hectare (57-square-kilometer or 22-square-mile) section of the Seymour River Valley in the southwest mainland area of British Columbia.

marijuana growing operation (grow op)   A marijuana farm, which may be outdoors or inside.

Metro Vancouver   A name that may refer to the city of Vancouver and the cluster of other cities, municipalities, and districts around it. Metro Vancouver is in the southwest mainland area of British Columbia and has a population of approximately 2.5 million people. Metro Vancouver is also often used as an abbreviation for the *Metro Vancouver Regional District*.

Metro Vancouver Regional District   A quasi-governmental organization that has control over many lands, resources, and services for communities in the Metro Vancouver region, including water, transit, and sewage. It is often referred to as *Metro Vancouver*.

midden   A discrete accumulation of trash.

natural levels   The stratigraphy in sediments. In archaeology, excavating by natural levels means that each distinct layer, as distinguished by the composition of the layer, is the primary unit of excavation. (Compare this, for example, to excavating according to *arbitrary levels*, in which the primary unit is a specific number of centimeters.) Natural levels are often difficult to distinguish without experience.

Nikkei   People of Japanese descent living outside of Japan. Those living in Canada are sometimes referred to as "Japanese Canadians."

nonjudgmental sampling   Unbiased sampling that relies on some form of randomness rather than the judgment or opinion of the person doing the sampling. It is also known as "probabilistic sampling." See also *judgmental sampling*.

Percheron   A breed of *draft horse*.

post-processual archaeology   An umbrella term for archaeology undertaken since the 1980s in scholarly but often nontraditional ways. This sort of archaeology often focuses on gender, ideology, and ethnicity, and it explicitly acknowledges bias. See also *processual archaeology*.

pothunter   A generic term applied to looters of archaeological sites. The term is derived from those searching for pottery, but it is widely applied to any looter looking for artifacts.

potsherd   A broken piece of pottery.

prehistoric   The period of time for which no written records exist. The transition from prehistory to history in the Metro Vancouver region occurs in the late 1700s when Europeans, with a system of writing, first began coming to the area.

privy   A small building used for relieving oneself of body waste, away from a residence. It is also known as an "outhouse." Usually a privy has a deep pit beneath the floor where the waste accumulates.

processual archaeology   Archaeology that emerged in the 1960s using scientific methods and focusing on explaining (rather than merely describing) culture change. See also *post-processual archaeology*.

public archaeology   Archaeology that actively engages the public.

rebar   A bar or rod, usually made of metal, used to strengthen and reinforce concrete. The word is derived from the phrase "reinforcing bar."

research design   A plan for research that includes determining its objectives and methods.

settler archaeology   In North America, archaeology focusing on people of European descent who arrived on the continent with the intention of living there. In the LSCR, "settlers" is a term appropriately used to describe the people of European descent living there. Nikkei living in the area are excluded from the category of settlers.

shingle bolts   Logs cut into sections of approximately 50 inches in length, which would eventually be used in the manufacture of shingles for building construction. Much of the logging in the LSCR was for shingle bolts.

shovelbums   Archaeological fieldworkers, often itinerant, who work on a project-to-project basis.

site datum   A single point to which all measurements at a site are tied. Site datum points are usually made permanent.

site integrity   A measure of how close the site is to its original condition. The assessment considers the impact of both natural and cultural processes that may have altered or disturbed the site.

site significance   A measure of how important a site is or has the potential to be. Significance is usually assessed by considering a site's importance to archaeology, history, the public, or a particular group (usually an ethnic group).

sterile   In archaeology, an absence of cultural remains. Archaeologists usually continue digging in an excavation unit until they reach a "sterile" level. Test pits without evidence of cultural remains are sterile.

survey   In archaeology, the search for archaeological sites. Sometimes this surveying is also called "reconnaissance."

temperate rain forest   A forest in the midlatitudes, generally with a mild climate, distinct seasonal changes, and heavy rains. These forests are often characterized by large trees with undergrowth on the forest floor of shrubs, ferns, and mosses.

total station   An electronic surveying instrument used at archaeological sites to measure distances, angles, and elevations from a fixed point.

Bibliography

Arcas Consulting. 1999. *Greater Vancouver Regional District Proposed Lower Seymour Conservation Reserve Recreational Pathway Archaeological Impact Assessment.* Report prepared for the Greater Vancouver Regional District. Report on file at the British Columbia Archaeology Branch, Victoria, BC.

Baxter, Jane Eva. 2017. *Archaeological Field Schools: A Guide to Teaching in the Field.* New York: Routledge.

Camp, Stacey. 2019. "Fieldwork and Parenting in Archaeology." In *Mothering from the Field: The Impacts of Motherhood on Site-Based Research*, edited by B.M. Muhammad and M. Neuilly, 27–42. Newark, NJ: Rutgers University Press.

Camp, Stacey. 2021. "The Future of Japanese Diaspora Archaeology in the United States." *International Journal of Historical Archaeology* 25 (3): 877–94. https://doi.org/10.1007/s10761-020-00564-6

Deetz, James. 1977. *In Small Things Forgotten: An Archaeology of Early American Life.* New York: Anchor/Doubleday.

Edgeworth, Matt, ed. 2006. *Ethnographies of Archaeological Practice.* Lanham, MD: AltaMira.

Gattuso, Reina. 2019. "The Japanese Ghost Town Buried Deep in a Canadian Forest." *Atlas Obscura*, September 23. https://www.atlasobscura.com/articles/japanese-immigrants-in-canada

Geiger, Andrea, ed. 2017. "Nikkei History." Special issue, *BC Studies* 192 (Winter). https://bcstudies.com/issue-single/bc-studies-no-192-winter-2016-2017/

Kagetsu, Tadashi J. 2017. *The Tree Trunk Can Be My Pillow: The Biography of an Outstanding Japanese Canadian.* Victoria, BC: University of Victoria.

Katz, Brigit. 2019. "Hidden Japanese Settlement Found in Forests of British Columbia." *Smithsonian Magazine*, September 3. https://www.smithsonianmag.com/smart-news/hidden-japanese-settlement-found-forests-british-columbia-180973028/

Klehm, Cara, Kurt Eifling, and Becca Peixotto, eds. 2021. "Health and Wellness in Archaeology: Improving Readiness and Response." Special issue, *Advances in Archaeological Practice* 9 (1). https://www.cambridge.org/core/journals/advances-in-archaeological-practice/issue/BF266BDF19C8682901C89C3E54917CEC

Lau-Ozawa, Koji, and Douglas Ross. 2021. "Critical Mass: Charting a Course for Japanese Diaspora Archaeology." *International Journal of Historical Archaeology* 25 (3): 577–91. https://doi.org/10.1007/s10761-020-00561-9

Leighton, Mary. 2020. "Myths of Meritocracy, Friendship and Fun Work: Class and Gender in North American Academic Communities." *American Anthropologist* 122 (3): 444–58. https://doi.org/10.1111/aman.13455

Muckle, Robert. 2017. "Archaeology of an Early Twentieth-Century Nikkei Camp in the Seymour Valley." *BC Studies* 192: 125–48. https://ojs.library.ubc.ca/index.php/bcstudies/article/view/187942/186353

Muckle, Robert. 2020a. "A Forgotten Settlement in the Seymour Valley." *British Columbia History* 53 (1): 13–16. BC Historical Federation. https://www.bchistory.ca/

Muckle, Robert. 2020b. "Archaeological Fieldwork." In *Encyclopedia of Global Archaeology*, edited by Claire Smith. Springer. https://doi.org/10.1007/978-3-030-30018-0_2843

Muckle, Robert. 2021. "Archaeology of Early Twentieth-Century Japanese Canadian Logging Camps in British Columbia." *International Journal of Historical Archaeology* 25 (3): 740–61. https://doi.org/10.1007/s10761-020-00578-0

Muckle, Robert, and Stacey Camp. 2021. *Introducing Archaeology*, 3rd ed. Toronto: University of Toronto Press.

Olson, Arv. 2004. *Shingles and Shells: A History of Fanny Bay*. Fanny Bay, BC: Fanny Bay OAP.

Richter, Brent. 2019. "Nikkei Secrets Unearthed on the Seymour." *North Shore News*, August 16. https://www.nsnews.com/local-news/nikkei-secrets-unearthed-on-the-seymour-3105344

Ross, Douglas. 2021. "A History of Japanese Diaspora Archaeology." *International Journal of Historical Archaeology* 25 (3): 592–624. https://doi.org/10.1007/s10761-020-00566-4

Roy, Patricia. 2003. *The Oriental Question: Consolidating the White Man's Province, 1914–1942*. Vancouver: UBC Press.

Sumida, Rigenda. 1935. "The Japanese in British Columbia." Master's thesis, University of British Columbia.

Sweet, Joni. 2020. "50 of the Greatest Archaeological Discoveries of All Time." *Stacker*, November 13. https://stacker.com/stories/4988/50-greatest-archaeological-discoveries-all-time

Voss, Barbara. 2021. "Documenting Cultures of Harassment in Archaeology: A Review and Analysis of Quantitative and Qualitative Research Studies." *American Antiquity* 86: 244–60. https://doi.org/10.1017/aaq.2020.118

Woodward-Reynolds, Kathleen. 1943. "A History of the City and District of North Vancouver." Master's thesis, University of British Columbia.

Index

Figures, tables, and boxes are indicated by page numbers in italics.